fresh and fast
vegan

amanda grant is a leading food editor in the United Kingdom. She appears regularly on radio and television, including a recurring slot on a daytime cooking show. Grant is the author of several books, including *The Powerfood Cookbook, Lunchbox,* and *Organic Baby Foods.* She lives in London.

Quick, Delicious, and
Creative Recipes to Nourish
Aspiring and Devoted Vegans

fresh and fast
vegan

amanda grant

Da Capo
LIFE
LONG

a member of the perseus books group

Designed by Pauline Neuwirth, Neuwirth & Associates, Inc.

Cataloging-in-Publication data for this book is available from the Library of Congress.

First published in the United States in 2002 under the title *Fresh & Fast Vegan Pleasures* Originally published in the United Kingdom in 1999 under the title *The New Vegan* by Metro Books, an imprint of Metro Publishing Limited. This edition published by arrangement.

The publisher would like to thank David Caruso and Linda Rao for their editorial contributions to the American edition.

Second Da Capo Press edition 2010
LCCN 2010932372
ISBN 978-0-7382-1429-0

Published by Da Capo Press, A Member of the Perseus Books Group
www.dacapopress.com

Note: The information in this book is true and complete to the best of our knowledge. This book is intended only as an informative guide for those wishing to know more about health issues. In no way is this book intended to replace, countermand, or conflict with the advice given to you by your own physician. The ultimate decision concerning care should be made between you and your doctor. We strongly recommend you follow his or her advice. Information in this book is general and is offered with no guarantees on the part of the authors or Da Capo Press. The authors and publisher disclaim all liability in connection with the use of this book. The names and identifying details of people associated with events described in this book have been changed. Any similarity to actual persons is coincidental.

Da Capo Press books are available at special discounts for bulk purchases in the United States by corporations, institutions, and other organizations. For more information, please contact the Special Markets Department at the Perseus Books Group, 2300 Chestnut Street, Suite 200, Philadelphia, PA 19103, or call (800) 810-4145, extension 5000, or e-mail special.markets@perseusbooks.com.

10 9 8 7 6 5 4 3 2 1

contents

introduction 1
metric conversions 4
the vegan diet and nutrition 5
stocking your pantry, fridge and freezer 9

starters ❖ 17

Spiced Nuts 18
Coriander Spiced Nuts 19
Hot and Spicy Popcorn 20
Roasted Baby Zucchini 21
Olives with Fresh Rosemary and Orange 22
Pureed Avocado Dip with Pickled Ginger and Wasabi 23
Lemon Tahini Dip 24
Vegetable Chips 25
Cayenne Chips 26
Melon with Red Wine and Mint Sauce 27
Melon with Toasted Seeds 28
Steamed Bok Choy with Soy Sauce and Toasted Seeds 29
Chili Pakoras with Chunky Tomato Chutney 30
Vegetables in a Crispy Chickpea Batter 32

Parsley and Garlic Pita Toasts   34
Pureed Chickpeas with Stir-Fried Vegetables   35
Warm Butter Bean Puree   36
Baked Asparagus with Garlic Croutons   38
Beets with Vinaigrette   39
Hot Grilled Sweet Potato with Watercress Salsa   40
Rich Mushrooms on Toast with Truffle Oil   42
Mushrooms with Peppercorns and Garlic   43
Crunchy Baked Tomatoes with Lime, Onion and Chili   44
Baby Mediterranean Tarts with Fresh Basil Puree   45
Fried Tomato Toasts   46
Blood Oranges with Red Onions, Black Olives and Fennel Dressing   47
Potatoes with Broad Beans and Mint Vinaigrette   48
Avocado with Beans and Cilantro   49
Roasted Apple, Onion and Sweet Potato Soup   50
Thai Pumpkin and Coconut Soup   52
Creamy Carrot and Ginger Soup with Curly Toasts   53
Tomato Soup with Cilantro Salsa   54
Corn, Coconut, Lime and Basil Soup   56
Wild Mushroom Soup   58
Roasted Squash Soup with Fresh Cilantro   59
Spicy Gazpacho Soup with Paprika Croutons   60
Vegetable Stock   62

snacks & light meals ❖ 63

Moroccan Spiced Couscous with Fruit   64
Griddled Red Onion Slices with Couscous   66
Warm Couscous with Garlic, Black Olives and Tomatoes   67
Bright Red Pepper Pesto Linguine   68
Fresh Ginger and Basil Pasta   69
Summer Pasta Salad   70
Roast Vine Tomatoes and Pasta   72
Rich Mushroom Sauce with Tagliatelle   73
Vivid Beet and Horseradish Gnocchi   74
Puree of Beans and Potatoes with Olive Oil   75
Samosas with Mango Chutney   76
Mediterranean Galette   78
Fennel and Ginger Tarts   79
Four-Onion Croustades   80
Fresh Broad Beans with Paprika and Lemon   81
Warm Tomato and Eggplant Stacks   82

Warm Lemon and Olive Oil Beans on Rosemary Mashed Potatoes   84
Warm Cumin and Coriander Spinach on Garlic Mashed Potatoes   86
Balsamic White Peach Salad with Parsley Shortcakes   88
Red Cabbage Relish with Parsley Mashed Potatoes   90
Papaya and Cilantro Salsa on Coconut Rice   91
Chili and Cilantro Corn Fritters with Tomato Sauce   92
Grilled Eggplant with Black Olive Dressing   94
Spanish Potato Gratin   95
Roasted Potatoes and Parsnips with Chestnuts and Sage   96
Salad of Ciabatta Croutons with Avocado, Grapefruit and Vinaigrette   97
Spicy Satay on White Bread   98
Basmati and Wild Rice Salad   99
Winter Green Salad with Very Garlicky Vinaigrette   100
A Very Modern Waldorf Salad   101

Pita Bread with Garlic Cream and Fresh Lime   104
Thai Vegetables in Fresh Herb Bread   105
Avocado Butter with Tomato Relish in Focaccia   106
Carrots with Mint and Lime Dressing in Pita Bread   107

Roasted Garlic Polenta with Sautéed Tomatoes   110
Tomato and Pine Nut Linguine with Caramelized Lemon   112
Gnocchi with Tomatoes and Fresh Mint   113
Mixed Mushrooms and Tofu Pasta   114
Spaghetti with Tomato Sauce   116
Roasted Garlic and Walnut Linguine   117
Thai Noodles with Chili and Lemon Grass Dressing   118
Vegan Sushi with Avocado and Cucumber   120
Red Cabbage with Sake on Rice Noodles   122
Tomato and Basil Risotto   123
Caramelized Fennel and Shallot Risotto   124
Moroccan Pilaf   125
Japanese Rice Bowl with Vegetables   126
Spring Vegetables with Saffron Basmati Rice   128
Spicy Vegetables and Coconut Cream   130
Juma's Special African Curry   132
Wontons with Chili Sauce   134

Chilied Spring Rolls with Dipping Sauce 136
Polenta with Beans 138
Sticky Golden Onion Tarts 139
Tuscan Tarts 140
Malaysian Vegetables 141
Grilled Vegetables on Lemon Grass Sticks with Coriander Basmati 142
Roasted Vegetables with Couscous and Lemon Pepper Oil 144
Potato Cakes with Peach and Lemon Grass Chutney 146
Moroccan Spiced Red Potato with Chickpeas 148
Mediterranean Potatoes with Olives, Herbs and Tomatoes 150
Eggplant and Potato Bake 151
Indian Vegetables 152
Balti 154
Stir-Fried Black Beans with Lime and Chili 156
Thai Green Vegetable Curry 158
Eggplant Butter with Sea Salt-Crusted Potatoes 160
Eggplant Slices with Lemon and Cilantro 162
New Potatoes and Small Peas with Pungent Green Sauce 163
Pacific Rim Coconut Curry 164
Crispy Polenta Peppers and Zucchini with Balsamic Vinegar 166
Roasted Red Onions and Wilted Spinach with Sweet Potatoes 167
Individual Crispy Porcini Bakes 168
Spicy Vegetable Rounds with Chunky Tomato Chutney 170
Moroccan-Style Chickpeas with Saffron Rice 172
Vegan Lasagna 174
Homemade Pizzas 176

desserts ❖ 179

Warm Hazelnut Scones with Fruit Salsa 180
Coconut Rice Pudding with Mango and Papaya 181
Moroccan Spiced Rice Pudding 182
Baked Pears and Ginger 184
Hot Poached Pears with Toffee Crisps 185
Poached Fruit in Lavender-Infused Syrup with Toffee Crisps 186
Fruit with Cardamom and Vanilla 187
Orange and Passionfruit Sorbet 188
Papaya and Coconut Sherbet 190
Coconut Ice Dessert with Chocolate Sauce 192
Lemon Sherbet Cups with Crushed Blueberries 194
Frozen Yogurt Crunch with Raspberry Sauce 195
Fresh Fruit in Wine with Basil 196

Strawberries with Black Pepper 197

Toffee Figs with a Glass of Brandy 198

Caramelized Oranges with Cranberries 199

Orange Custard with Cherry Jam 200

Plum and Cinnamon Crisp 201

Pancakes 202

Caramelized Peach and Almond Tart 203

Pecan and Butternut Squash Tart 204

Treacle Tart 206

Baked Bananas with Orange and Hazelnuts 207

Banana Flapjacks with Fresh Fruit Compote 208

Walnut Layer with Apple and Brandy Sauce 210

Sponge Cake with Strawberries and Lemon Balm 212

Chocolate Raspberry Hazelnut Cake 214

Apricot and Raspberry Cobbler 215

Crispy Cinnamon Bread Knots with Apricot Sauce 216

Winter Fruit Salad 218

menus 219
index 223

introduction

what an exciting challenge—writing a book of dairy-free vegetarian recipes! Although I am not exclusively vegan, I believe passionately in the benefits of eating the foods that make up a vegan diet to achieve optimum health and vitality.

why vegan?

The vegan diet is based on a wonderful variety of vegetables, fruits, nuts and seeds, grains and legumes, seasoned with fresh herbs and exotic spices from all over the world. Vegan diets avoid all meat, fish, poultry, animal milk and honey, as well as all animal-derived products and by-products.

There are many reasons why people are drawn to a vegan way of life. Although a minority of people begin eating a vegan diet for spiritual reasons, research shows that many vegans choose the diet because of animal rights issues or out of concern for the environment—global warming and the use of land, energy and water. Many people argue that using land for animal farming is inefficient compared with plant cultivation: Did you know that one-third of the grain we grow is fed to animals? A vegan diet requires just one-eighth of the land that's needed to provide food for a meat-based diet. In fact, there's a strong belief among many vegans that much of the world's food problem could be alleviated if land currently devoted to animal farming were turned over to plant cultivation.

In addition to animal and environmental reasons, some people choose to eat a vegan diet out of concern for their health. After all, public health organizations encourage us to eat at least five servings of fruit and vegetables daily, which speaks volumes for the virtues of a diet based on these ingredients.

why i wrote this book

As it happens, I also have personal reasons for writing this cookbook and encouraging others to incorporate vegan recipes into their everyday eating.

First, my background is based in food and nutrition. I have always had a passion for food, so it would seem logical that I write on this subject. In addition, I've spent a number of years researching diet and health, with a particular interest in cancer and food. (As you may know, there is a good deal of evidence linking poor diet to life-threatening diseases.) Because of the strong link between diet and health, we are continually being encouraged to increase our consumption of fruit and vegetables—the basic ingredients of a vegan diet.

Further, many people seem to suffer from some form of food intolerance, whether to dairy products or to meat, which makes finding appropriate and healthy recipes a challenge. I hope that the recipes in this book, which come out of my love of food and good health, will help readers with that challenge.

And finally, the joy that my new recipe ideas brought my late mother, who died in 1997 after a long, hard-fought battle with cancer, made me realize that other people would take delight in my creations as well. It is in my mother's memory that I write this book.

a word about my recipes

I spent a number of months developing a wide range of quick, simple and delicious recipes that can help you to live a healthy life and feel great, with more energy and vitality. You'll find that many of my recipes are influenced by world cuisine, a job made so much easier by the fabulous, continually evolving array of international ingredients available in supermarkets and local stores, particularly the foods of Japan and Morocco. The addition of some hot wasabi (Japanese horseradish) or a sprinkling of thinly sliced pickled ginger over a light noodle dish is tastebud-tingling stuff! Other Japanese ingredients such as dashi-konbu (a kind of seaweed) and sake also turn up in my recipes. Couscous, one of Morocco's gifts to the culinary world, plays a big role in this book. Having spent much time in France, Italy and Spain, I am also a great fan of the Mediterranean style of cooking, and these cuisines also influence the recipes in the chapters that follow.

I think it's important that both ardent carnivores and vegans alike take pleasure in dipping into this book and enjoying all the recipes. Only a few weeks ago, I had a few meat-eating friends over for supper and served a completely vegan menu: Everyone picked their plate clean and then requested my recipes! One guest even went so far as to say that he hadn't missed the meat. I know it was only one meal, but it's a start!

vegan meals—exciting and easy!

As you'll soon discover, it's a complete myth that meatless, dairy-free diets are necessarily dull or monotonous. But in order to avoid boredom, vegan meals must be well balanced. Even when you entertain friends who don't share your dietary interests, serving a vegan meal isn't a problem as long as you plan a satisfying menu. For those of you who find meal planning a struggle, or just want someone else to do the thinking for you, I have included menus at the end of the book.

Keep in mind that you can prepare vegan food fresh and fast—you don't need to focus on fancy nut loaves that demand five hours' preparation and cooking time. As you'll see, the recipes in this book illustrate that vegan food can be new and creative—or based on established favorites such as lasagna. Contrary to popular belief, vegans don't have to miss out on delicious, imaginative meals. So keep reading—and happy eating!

METRIC CONVERSIONS

- The recipes in this book have not been tested with metric measurements, so some variations might occur.
- Remember that the weight of dry ingredients varies according to the volume or density factor: 1 cup of flour weighs far less than 1 cup of sugar, and 1 tablespoon doesn't necessarily hold 3 teaspoons.

— General Formulas for Metric Conversion

Ounces to grams	⇒ ounces × 28.35 = grams
Grams to ounces	⇒ grams × 0.035 = ounces
Pounds to grams	⇒ pounds × 453.5 = grams
Pounds to kilograms	⇒ pounds × 0.45 = kilograms
Cups to liters	⇒ cups × 0.24 = liters
Fahrenheit to Celsius	⇒ (°F − 32) × 5 ÷ 9 = °C
Celsius to Fahrenheit	⇒ (°C × 9) ÷ 5 + 32 = °F

— Linear Measurements

½ inch = 1½ cm
1 inch = 2½ cm
6 inches = 15 cm
8 inches = 20 cm
10 inches = 25 cm
12 inches = 30 cm
20 inches = 50 cm

— Volume (Dry) Measurements

¼ teaspoon = 1 milliliter
½ teaspoon = 2 milliliters
¾ teaspoon = 4 milliliters
1 teaspoon = 5 milliliters
1 tablespoon = 15 milliliters
¼ cup = 59 milliliters
⅓ cup = 79 milliliters
½ cup = 118 milliliters
⅔ cup = 158 milliliters
¾ cup = 177 milliliters
1 cup = 225 milliliters
4 cups or 1 quart = 1 liter
½ gallon = 2 liters
1 gallon = 4 liters

— Volume (Liquid) Measurements

1 teaspoon = ⅙ fluid ounce = 5 milliliters
1 tablespoon = ½ fluid ounce = 15 milliliters
2 tablespoons = 1 fluid ounce = 30 milliliters
¼ cup = 2 fluid ounces = 60 milliliters
⅓ cup = 2⅔ fluid ounces = 79 milliliters
½ cup = 4 fluid ounces = 118 milliliters
1 cup or ½ pint = 8 fluid ounces = 250 milliliters
2 cups or 1 pint = 16 fluid ounces = 500 milliliters
4 cups or 1 quart = 32 fluid ounces = 1,000 milliliters
1 gallon = 4 liters

— Oven Temperature Equivalents, Fahrenheit (F) and Celsius (C)

100°F = 38°C
200°F = 95°C
250°F = 120°C
300°F = 150°C
350°F = 180°C
400°F = 205°C
450°F = 230°C

— Weight (Mass) Measurements

1 ounce = 30 grams
2 ounces = 55 grams
3 ounces = 85 grams
4 ounces = ¼ pound = 125 grams
8 ounces = ½ pound = 240 grams
12 ounces = ¾ pound = 375 grams
16 ounces = 1 pound = 454 grams

the vegan diet
and nutrition

there's increasing evidence that both vegan and vegetarian diets can help reduce our chances of developing cancer, heart disease and stroke, as well as diabetes, obesity, varicose veins, hemorrhoids, gallstones and constipation. This information alone was enough for me to study the subject and to ensure that I eat a lot of vegan meals and encourage my friends and family to do the same. Eating the right vegan foods simply means enjoying fresh, natural, organic and, where possible, raw produce rather than highly processed and refined foods.

An essentially natural food diet free of animal products is low in cholesterol, high in fiber, high in vitamins and minerals, low in saturated fat and, with a modest intake of sodium, or salt, fills all of our nutritional requirements. It is also the diet for which our digestive systems are best suited.

There's no need to panic about achieving the correct balance of vegan foods: Just eat a good mix of ingredients. The following descriptions will give you an idea of the sources of the essential nutrients that you should include in your diet. Once you understand the basics, incorporating vegan foods into your diet will become second nature.

❖ vitamins and minerals

A varied vegan diet will provide a good supply of vitamins and minerals, and there is an endless list of suitable fresh foods that are good sources of these nutrients. In particular, I consider fresh raw fruit and vegetables as nature's own vitamin and mineral pills.

A few other food sources worthy of a mention for their nutrient content—specifically the B vitamins—include almonds, cashews, pecans, pine nuts and dried apricots. Bean sprouts are also a good source of B vitamins. When beans or seeds, such as alfalfa, sprout, their levels of vitamin C and B-complex vitamins increase. The sprouting process also produces amino acids, converts fats into water-soluble vitamins and increases the food's enzyme activity.

And it's easy to incorporate bean sprouts into your diet—they're so versatile that you can add them to salads and sandwiches as well as to hot vegetable dishes. There are a wide range of beans and seeds that sprout. Have fun sprouting them yourself, or buy them from supermarkets or health food stores.

❖ vitamin b_{12}

In nature, vitamin B_{12} is found in animal products, but some nonanimal foods are fortified with the vitamin as well. For example, some seaweeds and freshwater algae are sources of vitamin B_{12}. To ensure an adequate supply of this vitamin, vegans need to eat B_{12}-fortified foods. But it's important to make sure that the product is free from animal sources of the vitamin: Check labels, or consult the manufacturer if you're in doubt. Some breakfast cereals are suitable, as is textured vegetable protein (TVP). Miso, a soybean paste, also contains vitamin B_{12}.

❖ vitamin d

The other vitamin that I need to mention is vitamin D, which is found in soy milk and fortified foods such as cereals; always check the manufacturer's label to ensure that an animal-free source of the vitamin has been used as a supplement. The most significant supply of vitamin D comes from sunlight, which, incidentally, does not need to be bright to be effective. Most people, including infants, require little or no extra vitamin D from food.

❖ iron

Too little dietary iron is often a cause of concern, because it can lead to anemia. Good sources of the mineral include whole grains, pumpkin and sesame seeds, nuts (cashews, walnuts, hazelnuts, Brazil nuts, pecans and peanuts), green beans, seaweed, dried fruit, molasses, chickpeas and red kidney beans. Green leafy vegetables such as spinach and watercress contain a lot of iron. But they also contain oxalic acid, which binds the iron, making a large proportion of it unavailable to the body. But here's some exciting news: Studies show that the iron status of vegans is usually normal and that iron deficiency is no more common among them than it is among the general population.

If you're concerned about getting enough iron, keep in mind that high levels of dietary vitamin C enhance iron absorption. So if you eat vitamin C–rich foods at the same time as iron-rich foods, you'll help your body to absorb more iron. For example, try drinking a glass of fruit juice—a good source of vitamin C—along with your iron-rich soy-milk-on-nutty-muesli breakfast.

❖ calcium

It is a misconception that cow's milk is the greatest source of calcium. People are often surprised to learn that this mineral is found in leafy green vegetables such as watercress, spinach, bok choy and kale. Fennel, leeks, broccoli, sesame seeds, almonds, Brazil nuts, soy milk, tahini (sesame seed paste), figs, seaweed and molasses are all sources of calcium. A cupful of broccoli contains as much calcium as seven fluid ounces of milk! I was delighted to read that some research shows that vegans and vegetarians tend to store and use calcium far more efficiently than people who eat meat.

❖ carbohydrates

Carbohydrates—starches and sugars—provide most of the body's energy. Good sources include breads, cereals, pasta, potatoes, vegetables and fruits, especially bananas. For optimum health and vitality, it's best to avoid refined sugars and sugary snacks.

❖ fat

The most obvious sources of fat include oils, seeds, nuts (and nut butters) and some grains and soy products.

❖ protein

Protein deficiency is virtually impossible if we consume sufficient calories to meet our needs. This rule even applies to children fed a vegan diet: Provided their energy needs are met, children thrive on diets in which the protein comes from a variety of different plant foods.

Most vegan diets incorporate at least some soy protein, which is equivalent in value to animal protein. Other protein sources include: grains and grain products, such as wheat, oats, rice, barley, buckwheat, millet, pasta and bread; peas; seeds, including pumpkin and sesame seeds; nuts, such as Brazil nuts, hazelnuts, almonds and cashews; yeast; wheat germ; dried or canned beans, such as red kidney and cannellini beans; and lentils.

As with most nutrients, the best way to consume the right amount of protein is to eat a wide variety of foods. For example, you might want to try eating these combinations: a mixture of nuts and seeds for a snack or sprinkled on salads; bean dishes with bread to combine vegetable and wheat proteins; cannellini beans and olives on fresh Italian bread for lunch; a chickpea dip with toasted pita bread; a rice dish with a handful of nuts scattered over the top. Eating foods such as these will help to ensure that you'll get a varied range of nutrients in your daily diet.

❖ essential ingredients

I hope the recipes in this book will show that it is relatively easy to cook and enjoy a varied vegan diet without having to spend hours in the kitchen. Similarly, you don't need to buy lots of unusual ingredients, because the basics are available from most good supermarkets, Asian groceries and health food stores. Wherever possible, buy fruit and vegetables in season—they're cheaper and often offer much more flavor.

to learn more

If you're interested in learning more about animal and animal-derived ingredients, you may want to read *Animal Ingredients A to Z*, second edition, from the E. G. Smith Collective, which is available at bookstores and through online booksellers.

stocking your pantry, fridge and freezer

some people think that vegan cooking is terribly complicated and involves a great deal of advance planning. While some advance planning is indeed necessary, having a well-stocked cupboard can help you create vegan meals in a flash. Here are some ingredients to keep on hand to help make your vegan cooking experiences as enjoyable and easy as possible.

stocking the pantry

It's a good idea to keep some nonperishable staples within easy reach. Here are some essentials.

❖ cans

Apart from beans and legumes, only three other canned ingredients work well in these recipes. Coconut milk is one of them. The coconut milk I'm talking about isn't the liquid inside the coconut—it's made from the grated flesh of fresh coconut. It is normally unsweetened. I tend to use the milk more often than the cream, which is pressed coconut with a thick, creamy texture, made with stabilizers and emulsifiers as well as water. The other two ingredients are corn and tomatoes, especially chopped plum tomatoes without added herbs or garlic.

❖ dried fruit

Dates, figs, apricots and raisins are delicious mixed into couscous- or rice-based dishes, or added to Moroccan-style chickpea stews. They are also excellent in puddings or for making sauces— pureed apricots with orange juice makes a wonderful sauce. Pack some dried fruit in your lunchbox, and nibble on that instead of chips.

❖ grains

Keep couscous, corn meal, soy flour, old-fashioned rolled oats and, if you wish, a packet of bulgur (cracked wheat) in the cupboard. I tend to prefer couscous to bulgur, and it's just as easy to use. Cover the grain in a warm stock, and leave it to soak for at least 15 minutes, until all of the liquid has been absorbed. Then add lots of herbs, olive oil and a few roasted vegetables, and you have a fabulous supper dish.

❖ jams

Buy fruit jams with a high fruit content and little sugar—they're great added to soy yogurt or spread thickly on scones or fruit breads.

❖ nuts and seeds

Pumpkin and sunflower seeds are delicious toasted and tossed over vegetable dishes or salads. A handful of nuts (especially almonds, cashews or Brazil nuts) that you've toasted and tossed in olive oil is always a quick treat. Both nuts and seeds transform rice dishes and hot vegetables into a complete meal.

❖ nut spreads

There are many nut spreads to choose from in the health food stores. Tahini (made from sesame seeds), peanut butter and cashew butter are my favorites. You can spread these nutty condiments on biscuits or bread for a quick snack, and you can use peanut butter to make a satay sauce (see Spicy Satay on White Bread, page 98).

❖ oils

Keep both light and extra virgin olive oils in your cupboard. The latter is great for salad dressings and drizzling over lightly cooked vegetables or finished dishes—or drizzled on fresh bread that has been rubbed with garlic. If you have room in the cupboard, also go for a bland peanut oil for frying and the faithful walnut oil for salad dressings—just mix it with a little lemon or lime juice. Sesame oil is strong in flavor, so you will only use a little at a time; it's great for drizzling over stir-fries or noodles.

❖ pasta

Keep a few favorites in the cupboard. Most varieties of pasta, including gnocchi, are made both with and without eggs, so check the ingredients list to make sure that eggs have been omitted.

❖ legumes

Chickpeas, cannellini beans, kidney beans, butter beans, broad beans and lentils are my favorites. Most of my recipes use canned varieties that require no soaking and precooking. Simply give them a good rinse under the faucet to remove any sugar or salt in the liquid.

❖ rice

I use basmati, Thai jasmine rice, Japanese sushi rice and arborio (or other risotto rice) in recipes throughout this book. Thai jasmine is a delicately flavored long-grain rice that is perfect with coconut or Thai-based curries. The grains of sushi rice, which comes mainly from California, are small, plump and often slightly soft and squishy when cooked. Sushi rice needs to be dressed with a vinegar and sugar solution while it is still warm so that it absorbs the dressing as it cools.

❖ salt

Sea salt flakes have such a wonderful taste that you'll be able to add less salt to your food than you normally would and get the same great flavor.

❖ sauces and pastes

Chutneys, whole-grain mustards, olive pastes, pesto and soy sauce are essentials. So is harissa, the North African chili paste that can transform couscous recipes in seconds. Always check the ingredients list to make sure the sauce doesn't contain animal products. Crushed tomatoes, though not strictly a sauce or paste, are also essential.

❖ seaweed

Seaweed provides an excellent source of vitamins A, C, D, E and K plus B vitamins, including B_{12}, which, as I mentioned earlier, is a vitamin that is rarely present in vegetables grown on land. Seaweed is also rich in minerals, especially iron. And foods such as dashi-konbu are great for adding a sweet flavor to rice. Nori is ideal for rice-wrapping: You could adapt the Vegan Sushi with Avocado and Cucumber (see page 120) and wrap nori around the rice balls. Alternatively, next time you're near a Japanese store, pick up a packet of seaweed, and add some to a vegetable stir-fry.

❖ spices

Keep a few whole spices such as green cardamom pods, coriander seeds, black peppercorns, cinnamon sticks, nutmeg and dried chilies in the cupboard, and grind them up when you need them. Other spices worth keeping are star anise and vanilla pods or extract—the recipe for Fruit with Cardamom and Vanilla on page 187 makes use of their full potential. Always use vanilla extract, which is the real thing, rather than vanilla essence, which is artificial. And don't forget saffron, a pretty and tasty friend. Quick tip: Add dried orange or lime zest to your pepper mill for a wonderfully fresh seasoning.

❖ sugars

Soft light or dark brown sugar, as well as turbinado sugar, lock in the natural molasses of sugar cane rather than refining it out. Once you've used these less-refined sugars you'll never cook with any other kind.

❖ vegetable stock

Homemade vegetable stock is best, but if you can't make your own, look for a vegan bouillon powder that's made with only organic products, including yeast extract, dried onions, dried carrots and dried parsley.

❖ vinegars

It's always a good idea to have balsamic and rice wine vinegars on hand. Keep in mind, though, that really good balsamic vinegars—those with sweet, rich, mellow flavors—often cost more than less flavorful types. And though cider and red wine vinegar are both useful ingredients in your kitchen, they aren't essential.

stocking the fridge

If you have a number of key ingredients in the fridge, you'll always be able to whip up a quick meal, whether it's pasta with chilies, ginger and herbs, or a salsa spread on partly baked bread and transformed into a pizza.

❖ chilies

A general guide is that long, thin chilies are hotter than those with broad shoulders. But some chile varieties prove otherwise, so when a recipe calls for chilies, just add a little at a time and taste as you go along—you can always add more. As soon as you add an ingredient such as coconut milk or any other high-fat liquid, the taste will become milder. Fresh chilies with wrinkled skins are hotter than smooth varieties. Dried chilies are the opposite: Wrinkled peppers are often sweeter than smooth peppers.

❖ ginger

This knobbly root will keep for several weeks in the vegetable drawer of your fridge. Just wrap it in paper towels and pop it into a paper bag first.

❖ herbs

I've used fresh herbs in all my recipes—a handful scattered over a dish adds so much color and flavor. If you can grow your own fresh herbs, do.

❖ lemon grass

Lemon grass, available at Asian markets and some larger grocery stores, is a staple of Southeast Asian cooking. Just remember to smash the thin end of the stick before using it to release the grass's citrus flavor.

❖ lemons and limes

Cut these citrus fruits into chunks, and griddle or fry them until golden. Serve them along with vegetable or pasta dishes.

❖ salsa

You'll never be caught short if you have a partly baked loaf of bread in your freezer and a good-quality salsa in your fridge—at least you'll be able to make a homemade pizza!

❖ soy milk and soy cream

Many different brands of soy milk and cream are available. Try a variety, and decide which ones you prefer.

❖ vegan margarine

There are many brands of margarine, all basically made from vegetable oils. But remember to check the label to make sure a margarine does not contain gelatin, whey, caseinates or other products derived from animals.

❖ vegetables

Leafy green vegetables—a packet of spinach leaves or a bag of bok choy—are great to keep on hand. Choose organic produce whenever possible.

stocking the freezer

I love my freezer; I can always dip into it and find something to turn into supper. The following are my essentials—but I always like to leave room for homemade shortcakes (see page 88).

❖ berries

Whip some berries in a food processor with soy ice cream or yogurt, or crush the berries and mix them with a sorbet. Serve this wonderful mixture in wine glasses.

❖ loaf of partly baked bread

Whoever pops in unexpectedly will be more than happy when they smell bread baking—and even more delighted to taste fresh, squishy bread topped with a little garlic and a drizzle of olive oil.

❖ sorbets and ice creams

There are many good fruit sorbets. Look for one with a high fruit content—but check the label to make sure it doesn't contain products derived from animals.

❖ young broad beans or small peas

With these tasty morsels, even if you don't have time to buy vegetables on your way home, you'll at least have something sweet and green on your plate for supper.

❖ pastry and crusts

Vegan puff, piecrust and filo pastry are freezer essentials. Seriously, who would make any of these from scratch when ready-made versions are available?

some extra ingredients

The following ingredients seem slightly too indulgent to be described as essentials, but are still great additions to any cook's cupboard.

❖ kaffir lime leaves

There is something almost magical about these leaves, which are available in Asian markets. They don't have the strong citric flavor of lime juice but are more aromatic. Experiment with them: Throw a couple into the water when you are cooking rice or pasta, or into a curry that uses lemon grass.

❖ pickled ginger

This wonderful Japanese ingredient adds a decorative kick to food. Avoid the bright pink kind—the color indicates the presence of a dye.

❖ wasabi

Wasabi is Japanese horseradish with real attitude. It may look like toothpaste in a squeezy tube, but don't be fooled! Put wasabi in a little bowl, and use it with caution.

❖ wines and spirits

A few bottles of white and red wine and a couple of liqueurs for fruit desserts are good cupboard ingredients. Just make sure that the products are vegan; animal-derived products are often used in the production of alcoholic beverages, in the fining or clearing process or as colorants and anti-foaming agents. Most spirits are acceptable (with the exception of malt whisky, some blended whiskies and Spanish brandies). I use a selection of spirits and organic wine in my recipes.

❖ a note about honey

Because bees produce honey it could be classified as an animal food. However, some vegans argue that making it does not cause any harm to the bees. The arguments for and against have caused disagreements; some vegans use honey, others do not. I have not used honey in the recipes in this book.

starters

spiced nuts

serves 6 (approx.)
preparation time: 5 minutes
cooking time: 5 minutes

this is a quick and easy nibble for serving with drinks. I was inspired to create the recipe after eating in an American restaurant where the chef had scattered something similar to these spicy nuts over a crisp green salad. The quantity is quite large—deliberately. Any leftover nuts will keep for up to three weeks in a screw-top jar and are perfect for satisfying hunger pangs or pepping up green salads or vegetables. Check the "hotness" of the nuts when they have cooled. If they are not spicy enough for you, heat a little more oil and add more chili powder, then return the nuts to the frying pan and cook them for a few minutes, tossing them to prevent burning.

1 tablespoon vegetable oil
1–2 teaspoons chili powder, preferably Kashmiri chili powder
1⅓ cup (about 10½ ozs.) mixed nuts; I recommend Bazil notes and almonds
mixed nuts, about 1⅓ (10½ ozs.) total; I recommend Brazil nuts and almonds
3–4 tablespoons soy sauce
sea salt

❖ Heat the oil in a wok or large frying pan. Add the chili powder and cook, stirring over a high heat for 1 minute. Add the nuts and toss them in the oil and chili powder until they are well coated. Fry the nuts for 1 minute, tossing and turning them as you do so.
❖ Add the soy sauce to the frying pan—it will sizzle as it hits the hot nuts. Cook over a high heat for 3 minutes or until all the sauce has evaporated, stirring frequently so that the nuts do not burn.
❖ Scatter a little salt over the nuts, then spread them on paper towels to drain and cool.

each serving contains:
Calories 345 • Protein 9g • Fat 32g (saturated 5.5g) •
Carbohydrates 3g • Fiber 3g • Calories from fat 86% • Excellent
source of vitamin E

coriander spiced nuts

serves 4
preparation time: 10 minutes
cooking time: 10–15 minutes

these make a wonderful change to a bowl of plain nuts, and there is something downright virtuous about saying that you made them. Whenever you use nuts in a recipe they should ideally be roasted to give the finished dish a really good nutty flavor. These nuts can be stored in a jar for up to three weeks— make sure it is airtight, or they will go soft.

1 cup (6 ozs.) sesame seeds
½ cup (1¾ ozs.) coriander seeds
½ cup (1¾ ozs.) hazelnuts
½ cup (1¾ ozs.) cashews
sea salt and freshly ground black pepper

❖ Preheat the oven to 350°F. Roast the sesame seeds and coriander seeds over moderate heat in a heavy skillet, turning or stirring frequently, for about 5 minutes, until the seeds are golden and starting to pop. Coarsely crush them using a pestle and mortar.
❖ Spread out the hazelnuts and cashews on a baking tray, and roast for 10–15 minutes until golden all over. Rub the skins off the hazelnuts. Coarsely chop all the nuts.
❖ Mix the nuts and seeds together, season with salt and pepper and serve.

each serving contains:
Calories 410 • Protein 12g • Fat 39g (saturated 5g) •
Carbohydrates 3g • Fiber 4.5g • Calories from fat 85% • Good
source of vitamin E

hot and spicy popcorn

serves 4
preparation time: 5 minutes
cooking time: 10–15 minutes

it is important to use a heavy saucepan or frying pan to prevent the popcorn from burning. A tight-fitting lid is also essential to ensure that the corn stays in the pan until all of it has popped. If you prefer a sweeter version, add a sweet spice such as cinnamon instead of cayenne and paprika, and replace the salt with a sprinkle of sugar. Serve the popcorn with drinks, or cool it and keep it in an airtight container until you are in the mood for a quick snack.

1 tablespoon vegetable oil
1 cup (3 ozs.) corn kernels
2 tablespoons olive oil
pinch of cayenne pepper
pinch of paprika
sea salt and freshly ground black pepper

❖ Heat the vegetable oil in a heavy saucepan or frying pan until it starts to simmer. Add enough corn kernels to form a single layer. Cover the pan. Listen carefully; when the kernels begin to pop, turn the heat down, and shake the pan gently every now and then. When the popping stops, take the pan off the heat, and tip the popcorn into a dish. Repeat with the remaining corn kernels.
❖ Toss the popcorn with the olive oil until well coated, then sprinkle with the cayenne pepper, paprika and salt and pepper to taste. Serve warm or cold.

each serving contains:
Calories 94 • Protein 1g • Fat 9g (saturated 1g) • Carbohydrates 3g • Fiber 0.3g • Calories from fat 82%

roasted baby zucchini

serves 4
preparation time: 15 minutes
cooking time: 15 minutes

here's an unusual snack to serve with drinks. If baby zucchini isn't available, use the same quantity of large ones, and slice the cooked vegetables before serving.

3 cups (14 ozs.) baby zucchini
½ cup (2½ ozs.) almonds
½ cup (2½ ozs.) white bread crumbs
sea salt and freshly ground black pepper
1 tablespoon extra virgin olive oil

❖ Preheat the oven to 400°F. Slice the zucchini in half lengthwise, and scoop out the seeds with a teaspoon.
❖ Dry-fry the almonds in a heavy frying pan over moderate heat, turning or stirring frequently, for 5 minutes or until they are golden.
❖ Put the almonds and bread crumbs in a bowl, season well with salt and pepper and mix thoroughly. Spoon the mixture into the zucchini halves, packing it in as tightly as possible, and drizzle the olive oil over them. Bake in the oven for 15 minutes. If you want the filling to look more golden, put the zucchini under a preheated grill for 2 minutes. Serve hot.

each serving contains:
Calories 225 • Protein 8g • Fat 14g (saturated 1g) • Carbohydrates 18g • Fiber 3g • Calories from fat 56% • Good source of vitamins C and E

olives with fresh rosemary and orange

serves 4
preparation time: 5 minutes, plus at least 1 hour marinating time

olives are always popular accompaniments to drinks. Presented this way, they look delicious—and are very quick to prepare. The longer you marinate them, the better. Leave out the garlic if you want the olives to have a subtle herb and citrus flavor. The strips of orange zest should be thick so that you can avoid them easily when serving.

approx. 1¼ cups (9 ozs.) mixed black and green olives, with pits
2 thick strips orange zest
3–4 sprigs of fresh rosemary
handful of fresh flat-leaf parsley, roughly chopped
1 garlic clove, sliced (optional)
3 tablespoons extra virgin olive oil

❖ Mix all the ingredients together in a serving bowl, and marinate for at least 1 hour.
❖ Remove the orange zest and rosemary sprigs.

each serving contains:
Calories 140 • Protein 0.5g • Fat 15g (saturated 2g) • Fiber 2g • Calories from fat 98%

pureed avocado dip with pickled ginger and wasabi

serves 4
preparation time: 15 minutes

in the tropics, the soft, lovely lime-green flesh of the avocado is known as "poor man's
butter." The Haas variety is
definitely my favorite. When
ripe, it is black and knobbly
on the outside, with a dense-
textured flesh that has a
nutty—almost hazelnut-like—
flavor. Avocados tend to discol-
or if they are prepared too far
in advance, so get all the ingredients for this recipe ready, and
prepare it just before you want
to serve the dip. Two Japanese
ingredients—pickled ginger
and wasabi paste—add a kick.
Serve with crudités and a bowl
of the pickled ginger.

3 large ripe avocados (preferably Haas)
2 tablespoons sweet pickled ginger
1 teaspoon wasabi paste
2 spring onions, trimmed and finely sliced
2 tablespoons sesame seeds
sea salt and freshly ground black pepper
1 tablespoon sunflower seeds

❖ Slice each avocado in half lengthwise, and remove the
  stone. Use a teaspoon to scoop the flesh into a small
  bowl. Add the pickled ginger, wasabi paste, spring
  onions and sesame seeds. Mash everything together,
  and season with salt and pepper.
❖ Spoon the dip into a serving bowl, and scatter the
  sunflower seeds over the top. Serve immediately.

each serving contains:
Calories 305 • Protein 4g • Fat 31g (saturated 7g) • Carbohydrates
2g • Fiber 5g • Calories from fat 92% • Good source of vitamins C
and E

lemon tahini dip

serves 4
preparation time: 15 minutes
cooking time: 5 minutes

tahini is a paste made from sesame seeds. Dips like this one are often served with Middle Eastern dishes such as falafel. The cumin seeds in this recipe are dry-fried and, as with all spices, this really enhances their flavor. I enjoy this dip spread on slices of fresh ripe plum tomato or with hot grilled vegetables (see page 35). It is also delicious served with Pita Toasts (see page 34). Add more than 1 teaspoon harissa paste if you wish—the more you add, the hotter the dip gets. The dip will keep for up to two days in the fridge.

1 teaspoon cumin seeds
2½ tablespoons (1¾ ozs.) tahini
juice of 1 lemon
1 teaspoon harissa paste (available in Middle Eastern grocery stores)
sea salt and freshly ground black pepper
4 fl. ozs. boiling water

❖ Dry-fry the cumin seeds in a heavy frying pan over moderate heat, turning or stirring frequently, for 3–4 minutes until golden. Coarsely crush the seeds using a pestle and mortar.

❖ Put the cumin in a bowl with the tahini, lemon juice, harissa and salt and pepper. Pour the boiling water over the mixture. Whisk thoroughly with a fork until well mixed. Cover the bowl with plastic wrap, and chill before serving.

each serving contains:
Calories 76 • Protein 2g • Fat 7g (saturated 1g) • Fiber 1g • Calories from fat 88%

vegetable chips

serves 4
preparation time: 20 minutes
cooking time: about 25 minutes

a very easy start to a meal. Big bowls of vegetable chips look great, taste delicious and are very simple to make. Use a vegetable peeler or sharp knife to cut the vegetables into the thinnest possible slices—aim for potato-chip size.

vegetable oil, for deep-frying
2 cups (7 ozs.) parsnips, thinly sliced
1 lb. sweet potatoes, peeled and thinly sliced
1 lb. raw beets, peeled and thinly sliced
sea salt
cayenne pepper (optional)

❖ Preheat the oven to 300°F. Line a plate or baking tray with paper towels. Half-fill a deep fryer or a deep, heavy saucepan with the vegetable oil, and heat to 375°F. To test the temperature, drop a cube of bread in the oil—it should brown within seconds.

❖ Carefully drop a handful of vegetable slices into the oil, and fry for 3–4 minutes, until they are golden and crisp. Remove the slices with a slotted spoon, drain them on the paper towels, then transfer them to the oven to keep warm. If you put too many vegetables into the oil at one time, the temperature of the oil will be lowered and the chips will be greasy and soggy when cooked.

❖ Repeat the process with the remaining vegetable slices.

❖ Transfer the chips to a warm serving dish, sprinkle with salt and cayenne pepper (if using) and serve.

each serving contains:
Calories 200 • Protein 3g • Fat 10g (saturated 1g) • Carbohydrates 26g • Fiber 5g • Calories from fat 45% • Good source of folic acid and vitamins A, C and E

cayenne chips

serves 4
preparation time: 15 minutes
cooking time: about 15 minutes

a bowl of spicy chips is a delicious way to start a casual supper. I fry them for a few minutes, drain them on paper towels and then fry them quickly again so that the chips are crisp on the outside and fluffy in the middle.

2 lbs. potatoes, peeled
8 teaspoons cayenne pepper
vegetable oil, for deep-frying
sea salt

❖ Preheat the oven to 300°F. Line a plate or baking tray with paper towels. Cut the potatoes lengthwise into ½″ slices, then cut the slices in half lengthwise. Sprinkle 3 teaspoons cayenne pepper over the slices.

❖ Half-fill a deep fryer or a deep, heavy saucepan with the vegetable oil, and heat to 375°F. To test the temperature, drop a cube of bread in the oil—it should brown within seconds.

❖ Carefully drop half the potato slices into the oil and fry for 4–5 minutes. Remove and spread them out to drain on paper towels. Heat the oil, to 375°F again, then return the chips to the deep fryer or saucepan for 1 minute. Spread them out on the paper towels, sprinkle with 1 teaspoon cayenne pepper and salt to taste, and transfer to the oven to keep warm. Repeat with the remaining potato slices.

❖ Transfer to a warm serving bowl, and serve.

each serving contains:
Calories 290 • Protein 5g • Fat 14g (saturated 1.5g) • Carbohydrates 39g • Fiber 3g • Calories from fat 43%

melon with red wine and mint sauce

serves 4
preparation time: 15 minutes
cooking time: 10 minutes

the contrast between the melon and the red sauce makes for a visually stunning dish. I like to use a canteloupe, but any melon in season will be fine provided it is fresh and ripe. Check for this by smelling it—it should have a wonderful aroma. I use red wine and confectioners' sugar for the sauce, but any combination of wine and sugar tends to perk up most fruit. If you are looking for a quick dessert or starter, choose a selection of seasonal fruit, drizzle some white wine and a sprinkling of confectioner's sugar over them, and serve.

3½ fl. ozs. dry red wine
2 tablespoons confectioners' sugar
2 fl. ozs. red wine vinegar
finely grated zest of 1 orange
large handful of fresh mint leaves, roughly chopped
freshly ground black pepper
1 large ripe melon
handful of fresh mint leaves, to serve

❖ Mix the wine and sugar in a saucepan, and heat gently until the sugar has dissolved. Let cool.
❖ Stir the vinegar, orange zest and mint into the wine syrup, and season to taste with the pepper.
❖ Cut the melon in half, and scoop out the seeds with a teaspoon. Cut each half lengthwise into 2 segments. Slice the flesh away from the skin of each segment by running a knife blade between the flesh and skin, and cut the flesh into long thin strips.
❖ Divide the melon strips among four plates, and drizzle a little of the sauce over them. Add a scattering of mint leaves, and serve with any remaining sauce.

each serving contains:
Calories 110 • Protein 1g • Fat less than 1g (no saturated fat) • Carbohydrates 22g • Fiber 1.3g • Calories from fat 2% • Excellent source of vitamin C

melon with toasted seeds

serves 4
preparation time: 2 minutes
cooking time: 8–12 minutes

a cantaloupe, or any melon in season, is fine for this recipe. The seeds are also delicious scattered over hot vegetables such as Steamed Bok Choy with Soy Sauce and Toasted Seeds (see page 31) or salads. Alternatively, do as I do and nibble on them while sipping a cool drink.

1 cup (7 ozs.) pumpkin seeds
4 tablespoons extra virgin olive oil
sea salt
freshly ground black pepper
1 cantaloupe

❖ Preheat the oven to 350°F. Mix the pumpkin seeds with the olive oil, and spread them on a baking sheet. Scatter a little salt over them, and bake for about 10 minutes, until lightly toasted. Remove the seeds from the oven, sprinkle with pepper and more salt, and let cool.

❖ Cut the melon in half, and scoop out the seeds with a teaspoon. Cut each half lengthwise into 2 segments. Slice the flesh away from the skin of each segment by running a knife blade between the flesh and skin, and cut the flesh into bite-size chunks.

❖ Divide the melon chunks among four plates, scatter the crunchy seasoned seeds over them, and serve.

each serving contains:
Calories 495 • Protein 13g • Fat 41g (saturated 6g) • Carbohydrates 18g • Fiber 3.5g • Calories from fat 75% • Good source of vitamin C

steamed bok choy with soy sauce and toasted seeds

serves 4
preparation time: 15 minutes
cooking time: 15 minutes

a bowl of steaming soy greens and toasted seeds is an excellent—and simple—way to begin a supper. (Don't forget the chopsticks!) Bok choy is available in supermarkets. The leaves look a little like spinach and taste delicious raw or quickly cooked.

1 cup (7 ozs.) pumpkin seeds
4 tablespoons extra virgin olive oil
sea salt and freshly ground black pepper
2 heads of bok choy
2 tablespoons peanut oil
1 tablespoon chopped garlic
2 tablespoons soy sauce

❖ Preheat the oven to 350°F. Mix the pumpkin seeds with the olive oil, and spread them on a baking sheet. Scatter a little salt over them and bake for about 10 minutes, until lightly toasted. Remove the seeds from the oven, sprinkle with pepper and more salt, and let cool.

❖ Slice each head of bok choy down the middle from the top of the leaves to the stalk, then slice each half into thin strips.

❖ Heat the oil in a wok or large frying pan. Add the garlic, and fry gently for a few minutes, then stir in the soy sauce. Add the bok choy and toss the strips in the garlic and soy sauce until they are well coated and the bok choy has wilted slightly.

❖ Divide the greens among four warm bowls, scatter the toasted seeds over them, and serve.

each serving contains:
Calories 70 • Protein 2g • Fat 6g (saturated 0.6g) • Carbohydrates 2g • Fiber 1g • Calories from fat 76% • Good source of vitamin C

chili pakoras
with chunky tomato chutney

serves 4
preparation time: 20 minutes
cooking time: about 20 minutes

these vegetables fried in batter are crispy, hot and simple to make. The vegetables must be cut into bite-sized pieces so that they are easy to eat—especially important if you wish to serve them as canapés. The water for the batter must be very cold, so put it in the fridge to chill before you start the recipe. Garam masala is a classic Indian spice mix usually made from cinnamon, cloves, black pepper, coriander, cardamom, and cumin, and can be found at better supermarkets and specialty grocers. Gram flour is also known as chickpea flour.

2 teaspoons cumin seeds
2 teaspoons coriander seeds
2 teaspoons dried chili flakes
2 tablespoons vegetable oil
1½ cup (6 ozs.) gram flour
2 teaspoons garam masala
3 teaspoon sea salt
7 fl. ozs. chilled water
½ handful of fresh mint leaves, roughly chopped
½ handful of cilantro, roughly chopped
vegetable oil, for deep frying
1¼ lbs. mixed vegetables, such as mushrooms, cauliflower, okra, zucchini, cut into bite-size pieces
Chunky Tomato Chutney (see page 170)

❖ Preheat the oven to 300°F. Dry-fry the cumin seeds, coriander seeds and chili flakes in a heavy saucepan over moderate heat, turning or stirring frequently, for a couple of minutes until the seeds begin to pop. Coarsely crush the spices using a pestle and mortar.

❖ Heat the oil in a frying pan. Add the spices, and stir-fry them over moderate heat for 2 minutes to "cook off" the spice flavor.

❖ Line a plate or baking tray with paper towels. Mix the gram flour, garam masala and salt together in a bowl. Mix in the spice mixture, then gradually add chilled water to make a coating batter, beating vigorously with a wooden spoon or a balloon whisk to remove any lumps. Stir in the mint and cilantro. Leave the batter to stand for about 30 minutes.

❖ Heat the oil to about 375°F in a deep fryer or deep, heavy saucepan. To test the temperature, drop a little batter into the oil—it should sizzle immediately. When the oil is hot enough, dip 3 or 4 pieces of vegetable in the batter, then put them carefully in the oil and fry for about 4 minutes, or until they are golden brown. Drain the slices on the paper towels, then transfer them to the oven to keep warm. Repeat the process with the remaining vegetables.

❖ Serve the pakoras hot with a bowl of Chunky Tomato Chutney (page 170) as an accompaniment.

each serving contains:
Calories 215 • Protein 12g • Fat 9g (saturated 1g) • Carbohydrates 23g • Fiber 6g • Calories from fat 36%

vegetables in a
crispy chickpea batter

serves 4
preparation time: 10 minutes
cooking time: about 20–30 minutes

the batter will keep for 3–4 days in the fridge; you may need to add just a little water to thin it down slightly before using it. Adding paprika and cayenne just before the vegetables are served looks attractive and gives the batter that extra burst of flavor. You could always serve these crispy vegetables with Chunky Tomato Chutney (see page 170). The water for the batter must be very cold, so put it in the fridge to chill before you start the recipe.

1¾ cups (7 ozs.) chickpea flour
1 garlic clove, crushed
2 teaspoons cumin seeds
½ teaspoon turmeric
½ teaspoon baking powder
sea salt and freshly ground black pepper
2 tablespoons olive oil
12 fl. ozs. chilled water
vegetable oil, for deep-frying
1½ lb. mixed fresh vegetables, such as broccoli, cauliflower and zucchini, cut into bite-sized pieces
1 teaspoon cayenne pepper
1 teaspoon paprika

❖ Preheat the oven to 300°F. Line a plate or baking tray with paper towels. Mix the chickpea flour, garlic, cumin seeds, turmeric, baking powder and salt and pepper together in a bowl. Mix in the olive oil, then gradually add 12 fl. ozs. chilled water, or enough to make a coating batter. Beat vigorously with a wooden spoon or a balloon whisk to remove any lumps. Let the batter stand for about 30 minutes.

❖ Heat the oil to about 355°F in a deep fryer or deep, heavy saucepan. To test the temperature, drop a little batter into the oil—it should sizzle immediately. When the oil is hot enough, dip 3–4 pieces of vegetable in the batter, then put them carefully in the oil. Fry for about 4 minutes, or until they are golden brown. Drain them on the paper towels, and transfer them to the oven to keep warm. Repeat the process with the remaining vegetables.

❖ Transfer the vegetables to a warm bowl. Sprinkle the cayenne pepper, paprika and additional salt and pepper to taste over them. Toss lightly, and serve.

each serving contains:
Calories 400 • Protein 14g • Fat 25g (saturated 3g) • Carbohydrates 29g • Fiber 7g • Calories from fat 50% • Good source of folic acid and vitamin C

parsley and garlic pita toasts

serves 4
preparation time: 10 minutes
cooking time: 10 minutes

these toasts are a lighter version of garlic bread. I can guarantee that everyone you serve them to will love them. As with many of the other starters, they can be served with a soup or salad to make a lunch dish.

4 large pitas
3 tablespoons extra virgin olive oil
3 garlic cloves, crushed
handful of fresh flat-leaf parsley, roughly chopped

❖ Preheat the oven to 350°F. Slice each pita bread in half lengthwise, then cut each half into 4 or 5 strips. Place in a single layer on a baking tray, and bake for 10 minutes, until golden and crispy.
❖ Heat the oil in a frying pan. Add the garlic, and fry gently for a few minutes until softened. Drizzle the garlicky oil over the pita slices, and scatter the parsley over them.

To make **spicy pita toasts,** follow the recipe above, but replace the garlic with $1/2$ teaspoon cayenne pepper and 1 teaspoon paprika.

each serving contains:
Calories 300 • Protein 7g • Fat 12g (saturated 2g) • Carbohydrates 43g • Fiber 1.5g • Calories from fat 36%

pureed chickpeas
with stir-fried vegetables

serves 4
preparation time: 10 minutes
cooking time: 10 minutes

One cup of cooked chickpeas provides one quarter of an adult's daily protein requirement, one and a half times the folic acid requirement, half the iron and one fifth of the zinc. This puree also makes a great dip served with strips of toasted pita bread or potato chips.

approx 1¾ cups (14½ ozs.) canned chickpeas
1 garlic clove, roughly chopped
juice of ½ lime
3 tablespoons extra virgin olive oil
sea salt and freshly ground black pepper
handful of freshly chopped flat-leaf parsley
olive oil, for brushing
1 cup (4 ozs.) asparagus
1 cup (4 ozs.) baby corn
1 cup (4 ozs.) baby carrots

❖ Drain the chickpeas, and reserve half their liquid. Put the chickpeas, reserved liquid, garlic, lime juice and oil in a food processor, and process to a smooth puree. Season with salt and pepper, and mix in the freshly chopped parsley.

❖ Brush a griddle or heavy frying pan with a little oil, and heat it until very hot. Add the vegetables. Cook them, turning frequently, for 5 minutes or until golden.

❖ Serve the vegetables warm with the soft, creamy puree as an accompaniment.

each serving contains:
Calories 285 • Protein 10g • Fat 17g (saturated 2g) •
Carbohydrates 24g • Fiber 6g • Calories from fat 55% • Good source of vitamin A

warm butter bean puree

serves 4
preparation time: 15 minutes
cooking time: 20 minutes

it makes a welcome change to serve a warm, rather than chilled, dip. This puree is always a big hit. Serve it with fingers of hot toast or sea salt kettle chips. It also goes well with polenta, griddled vegetables or mashed potatoes. The cayenne pepper adds quite a kick, so if you feel the dip needs a sprinkling of color before serving, it is advisable to dust a little paprika, rather than extra cayenne, over the top.

2 cups (14½ ozs.) canned butter beans, drained
1 large potato, about 1 cup (8 ozs.), peeled and cut into chunks
1 bay leaf
4 tablespoons olive oil
1 medium-size onion, chopped
1 tablespoon cayenne pepper
3 garlic cloves, crushed
1 tablespoon lemon juice
sea salt and freshly ground black pepper

to serve
pinch of cayenne pepper (optional)
handful of cilantro leaves, roughly chopped

❖ Mash the beans into a coarse puree, and set aside.
❖ Bring a small saucepan of water to a boil, add the potato chunks and bay leaf, and simmer for 10–15 minutes, until the potato chunks are tender. Drain, discard the bay leaf, and return the saucepan to the heat. Dry the potato chunks over very low heat, shaking the pan gently, then mash them.
❖ While the potato chunks are boiling, heat 1 tablespoon of the oil in a frying pan, Fry the onion, cayenne pepper and 2 garlic cloves for about 10 minutes, or until the onion is soft. Add the pureed beans and mashed potatoes to the onion, and mix well. Warm the mixture through over low heat, stirring every now and then to make sure the puree doesn't stick to the pan.

❖ Beat the remaining garlic and olive oil into the puree, add the cilantro, and season to taste with the lemon juice, salt and pepper. Dust with a sprinkling of cayenne pepper, if using, and serve warm.

baked asparagus
with garlic croutons

serves 6
preparation time: 15 minutes
cooking time: 20 minutes

it is not surprising to learn that asparagus has been the pride of the vegetable garden since the Renaissance. Every way I cook it, I love it. This recipe looks stylish, is simple to make and is a wonderful starter, especially when the asparagus is served with fresh little garlic croutons. Avoid large, tasteless spears; go for young ones that are full of flavor. Fresh spears are firm, with tightly closed scales on the tips.

1 lb. fresh asparagus
2 tablespoons olive oil
3 cups (8 ozs.) mushrooms
freshly ground black pepper
handful of fresh flat-leaf parsley leaves

for the croutons
3 slices white bread, about 1″ thick
2 garlic cloves, crushed
4 tablespoons extra virgin olive oil

❖ Preheat the oven to 400°F. Break the tough ends off the asparagus (they should snap quite easily).
❖ Bring a saucepan of water to a boil, add the asparagus spears and simmer for 3–4 minutes. They must remain firm, not become tender. Drain the spears well on paper towels for a few minutes, then transfer them to a shallow ovenproof dish.
❖ Heat the olive oil in a frying pan, and sauté the mushrooms for 5–6 minutes, until they are brown and soft. Slice each mushroom diagonally, and place the slices on top of the asparagus. Drizzle the pan juices over the asparagus and mushrooms.
❖ To make the croutons: Place the cut bread on a baking tray in a single layer. Mix the garlic and extra virgin olive oil together in a bowl, and drizzle the mixture over the bread cubes. Bake in the oven for 10 minutes or until golden, turning the croutons once.
❖ Divide the baked asparagus between 6 warm serving plates. Scatter the croutons, pepper and a few parsley leaves over them, and serve immediately.

each serving contains:
Calories 250 • Protein 7g • Fat 12g (saturated 2g) • Carbohydrates 28g • Fiber 2.5g • Calories from fat 45%

beets with vinaigrette

serves 4
preparation time: 15 minutes
cooking time: 2–3 minutes

raw beets are packed with vitamin C—most of which is lost, along with its wonderful color, when the vegetable is boiled. I hope this recipe will help you to enjoy this root in its raw and attractive state. I have added a little fresh apple—my first choice is always the sweet Cox. Beets have a wonderful affinity with this fruit, which accentuates their natural sweetness and provides a little much-needed acidity. I have also added some walnuts and walnut oil, which both complement, and contrast with, the beets' flavor and texture. Use an extra tablespoon of olive oil if you do not have walnut oil.

pinch of sea salt
pinch of freshly ground black pepper
½ teaspoon Dijon mustard
2–4 tablespoons white wine vinegar, depending on how tart you like your vinaigrette
3 tablespoons olive oil
1 tablespoon walnut oil
2 large raw beets
3 sweet eating apples
½ cup (1¾ ozs.) walnuts
large handful of fresh arugula
large handful of watercress

❖ Mix the salt, pepper and mustard into the vinegar. Stir until the salt has dissolved, then gradually whisk in the olive and walnut oils with a fork.

❖ Peel the beets, cut each one into large chunks and grate them. Peel, core and grate the apples. Combine the beets and apples. Add the vinaigrette, and mix well. Set aside.

❖ Dry-fry the walnuts in a heavy frying pan, turning or stirring frequently, until golden. Allow the nuts to cool a little, then chop them roughly.

❖ Divide the arugula and watercress among four serving plates, and spoon the beets on top. Scatter the walnuts over the beets, and serve.

each serving contains:
Calories 195 • Protein 2g • Fat 19g (saturated 2g) • Carbohydrates 3g • Fiber 1g • Calories from fat 90% • Good source of vitamin C

hot grilled sweet potato
with watercress salsa

serves 4
preparation time: 15 minutes
cooking time: 30 minutes

watercress

is a favorite ingredient of mine, because of its peppery flavor and crunchy texture. Also, each leaf is packed with vitamins and minerals. I think it is underused and underrated in our cooking today—arugula seems to appear far more often on restaurant menus. Watercress adds color, texture and a spicy kick to this crispy salsa, as it does to other cold dishes. It is also great in hot dishes, especially stir-fries. Add it just before the end of cooking so that the pretty green leaves have only enough time to wilt.

6 ripe plum tomatoes
½ cucumber, unpeeled
big bunch of watercress, roughly chopped
3 tablespoons olive oil
juice of ½ lime
½ red chili pepper, seeded and chopped
4 medium-size sweet potatoes, unpeeled
olive oil, for brushing
sea salt and freshly ground black pepper

❖ Put the tomatoes in a bowl, and cover with boiling water. After 20 seconds in the boiling water, plunge them straight into cold water. Drain, skin and chop the tomatoes.
❖ Cut the cucumber in half lengthwise, scoop out the seeds with a teaspoon and dice the flesh. Mix the cucumber with the tomatoes and watercress and transfer to a serving bowl.
❖ Put the 3 tablespoons olive oil, lime juice and chili pepper into a screw-top jar, and shake well to blend the ingredients. Drizzle this dressing over the salsa. Cover the bowl with plastic wrap, and chill until needed.
❖ Gently scrub the potatoes to clean them. Bring a large saucepan of water to a boil, add the potatoes and simmer for about 20 minutes, until tender. To test, stick the point of a sharp knife into a potato—it should just go through the middle. Drain, and let cool.

❖ Cut the potatoes into 1″ slices. Brush a little olive oil on both sides of each slice, and sprinkle with salt and pepper. Heat a griddle pan or heavy frying pan until hot, and cook the potato slices for 2 minutes on each side, until golden brown.

❖ Divide the potatoes among four warm bowls, top with the crispy watercress salsa and serve.

each serving contains:
Calories 330 • Protein 5g • Fat 15g (saturated 2.4g) •
Carbohydrates 47g • Fiber 7g • Calories from fat 41% • Excellent
source of vitamins C, A and E • Good source of iron

rich mushrooms
on toast with truffle oil

serves 4
preparation time: 15 minutes, plus 20 minutes standing time
cooking time: 15 minutes

I can almost predict that whenever I go to a restaurant in autumn I will order a vegetarian dish that has more than its fair share of wild mushrooms. There is something quite magical about chanterelles and porcini—they add a wonderfully intense flavor to other ingredients. Although the price for these delicacies may be high, the consolation is that you only need a few to have a really dramatic impact on a finished dish. I have chosen to use dried porcini in this recipe, but morels are just as good. Drizzle the truffle oil—or a little extra virgin olive oil if truffle oil is too expensive—around each plate to finish the dish. Remember, you eat with your eyes!

½ cup (1 oz.) dried porcini mushrooms
(10 fl. ozs.) boiling water
3¼ cups (9 ozs.) portobello mushrooms
2 cups (5½ ozs.) white mushrooms
3 tablespoons extra virgin olive oil
2 garlic cloves, sliced
4 slices fresh white bread

to serve
handful of fresh flat-leaf parsley, chopped
2 teaspoons truffle oil

❖ Cover the porcini mushrooms with the boiling water, and let soak for 30 minutes. Drain, and roughly chop the porcini.
❖ Cut the portobello and white mushrooms into thick slices. Heat the oil in a frying pan, Add the garlic and fry, stirring frequently, for 1 minute over low heat without browning. Add the sliced portobello and white mushrooms and fry, stirring, for 1 minute. Add the chopped porcini, and fry for an additional 10 minutes, stirring now and then.
❖ While the mushrooms are cooking, toast the slices of bread.
❖ Put a slice of toast on each of 4 warm plates, and divide the mushrooms between them. Scatter chopped parsley over the mushrooms, drizzle a little truffle oil around each plate and serve immediately.

each serving contains:
Calories 200 • Protein 7g • Fat 11g (saturated 5g) • Carbohydrates 19g • Fiber 2.5g • Calories from fat 51%

mushrooms
with peppercorns and garlic

serves 4
preparation time: 10 minutes
cooking time: 15 minutes

everyone

loves garlic mushrooms, and this recipe takes that familiar dish one step further. It is inspired by the spices I saw growing in Zanzibar. There are so many that I want to incorporate in my recipes, and here I use lots of red and green peppercorns, which differ in color and flavor simply because of the time when they are picked. Unlike some other cultivated mushrooms, shiitake have a very distinctive flavor and texture that can add a little excitement to other fresh cultivated mushrooms. This makes a delicious starter served with fresh baked rolls—or a main course when it is accompanied by a pile of steaming mashed potatoes. Use a mixture of black and white peppercorns if red and green ones are unavailable.

1 teaspoon mixed red and green peppercorns
1½ cups (4½ ozs.) shiitake mushrooms
1½ cups (4½ ozs.) button mushrooms
1½ cups (4½ ozs.) portobello mushrooms
2 tablespoons olive oil
1 large onion, sliced
2 garlic cloves, crushed
5 fl. ozs. vegetable stock
1–2 dashes of Tabasco sauce
handful of cilantro, roughly chopped, to serve

❖ Dry-fry the peppercorns in a heavy frying pan over moderate heat, turning or stirring frequently, for 2 minutes or until they start to pop. Coarsely crush the peppercorns using a pestle and mortar.
❖ Tear the shiitake mushrooms into strips. Slice the button mushrooms into quarters and the portobello mushrooms into thin strips.
❖ Heat the oil in a frying pan, and fry the onion over moderate heat for 5 minutes, or until softened. Add the garlic and crushed peppercorns, and fry for an additional 2 minutes. Add the mushrooms, and fry for a further 5 minutes.
❖ Heat the stock until simmering, and pour it over the mushrooms. Simmer the mixture for 2 minutes, or until the stock has evaporated. Add Tabasco sauce to taste. Scatter cilantro over the mushrooms, and serve immediately.

each serving contains:
Calories 80 • Protein 3g • Fat 6g (saturated 0.85g) • Carbohydrates 3.5g • Fiber 1g • Calories from fat 70%

crunchy baked tomatoes
with lime, onion and chili

serves 4
preparation time: 10 minutes
cooking time: 10 minutes

it is important that the tomatoes have lots of flavor— all too often, the larger they are, the less flavor they have. If this is the case, use twelve smaller tomatoes bursting with flavor rather than eight large ones. Ever since I drizzled lime juice over tomatoes before roasting them I have found the combination hard to beat. This makes a lovely starter served with fresh bread or a wonderful main course accompanied by hot potatoes or polenta.

8 or 12 medium-size vine-ripened tomatoes
sea salt and freshly ground black pepper
2 bunches of spring onions, finely chopped
1 small red chili pepper, seeded and finely chopped
1" piece of fresh ginger, peeled and finely chopped
2 garlic cloves, finely chopped
2 tablespoons fresh basil leaves, roughly torn
3½ tablespoons (1¾ ozs.) plain potato chips
juice of 1 lime
juice of 1 orange
2 tablespoons extra virgin olive oil

❖ Preheat the grill to high. Slice off the tops of the tomatoes, and scoop out the seeds and juice with a teaspoon. Turn the tomatoes upside down as you do so to allow them to drain slightly. Dry the insides of the tomatoes with paper towels, and season with salt and pepper.

❖ Combine the spring onions, chili peppers, ginger, garlic and basil, and mix well. Fill the tomatoes with this mixture, then crumble a few chips over the mixture. Drizzle the lime and orange juices and olive oil over the top of each tomato.

❖ Place on the grill for about 2 minutes, until the tomatoes are warm and the onion mixture is just turning golden. Serve immediately.

each serving contains:
Calories 210 • Protein 3g • Fat 16g (saturated 3.5g) •
Carbohydrates 14g • Fiber 3g • Calories from fat 69% • Excellent source of vitamin C • Good source of vitamins A and E

baby mediterranean tarts
with fresh basil puree

serves 4
preparation time: 15 minutes
cooking time: 15 minutes

these tarts are a perfect example of how to combine ease with stylish presentation. Make sure you have plenty of fresh basil leaves to scatter over them just before serving. The tarts can be prepared in advance, then covered with plastic wrap until you are ready to bake them.

3 garlic cloves, sliced
30 fresh basil leaves
3 tablespoons extra virgin olive oil
juice of 1 lemon
sea salt and freshly ground black pepper
11″ x 9″ sheet of frozen ready-rolled puff pastry, thawed
4 tablespoons crushed tomatoes
10 pitted black olives, sliced
handful of fresh basil leaves, roughly torn

❖ Preheat the oven to 425°F. Put the garlic and fresh basil in a food processor, and process to a paste. Add the oil and lemon juice, and process the mixture until blended. Alternatively, chop the garlic and fresh basil, and mix thoroughly with the oil and lemon juice. Season to taste with salt and pepper.

❖ Use a round cutter or egg cup to cut out twenty 1½″ circles of pastry. Put the circles straight onto a baking sheet, and prick them all over with a fork. Spoon a little of the crushed tomatoes onto each pastry circle, top with a few olive slices and season to taste with salt and pepper. Drizzle 1 teaspoon basil puree over each tart.

❖ Put the tarts in the oven, and bake for 10–12 minutes, until risen and golden. Divide them among four warm plates, and drizzle 1 teaspoon basil puree over them. Scatter a few basil leaves on top, and serve hot. For a really dramatic look, drizzle the remaining basil puree around each plate.

each serving contains:
Calories 290 • Protein 3g • Fat 22g (saturated 1g) • Carbohydrates 21g • Fiber 0.5g • Calories from fat 68%

fried tomato toasts

serves 4
preparation time: 10 minutes
cooking time: 10 minutes

there is something quite delicious about hot fried bread topped with soft cool tomatoes, and the addition of fresh basil and black pepper takes it into a different world. Some people are lucky enough to enjoy picking fresh, sun-ripened tomatoes straight from the vine, when the red and round fruit is at its sweetest. For those of us who are not so fortunate, many types are available nowadays, so it is slightly easier to find a variety that has both flavor and texture. Choose one with a skin that is not too tough or thick and a flesh that is succulent.

8 ripe plum tomatoes
4 slices fresh herb bread *or* white bread
vegetable oil, for frying
large handful of fresh basil leaves
sea salt and freshly ground black pepper
extra virgin olive oil, to drizzle

❖ Put the tomatoes in a bowl, and cover with boiling water. After 20 seconds in the boiling water, plunge them straight into cold water. Drain, skin and roughly chop the tomatoes. Set aside.
❖ Cut each slice of bread into quarters. Heat a little vegetable oil in a large frying pan, and fry the bread quarters until they are golden on both sides.
❖ Divide the bread quarters among four warm serving plates, and top them with the tomatoes. Stack about 6 basil leaves together, roll them into a cigar shape and cut into thin strips. Repeat with the remaining basil leaves. Scatter the strips of basil over the tomatoes, and season well with salt and pepper. Drizzle a little extra virgin olive oil around each plate, and serve.

each serving contains:
Calories 245 • Protein 4.5g • Fat 15g (saturated 2g) •
Carbohydrates 23g • Fiber 2.5g • Calories from fat 57% • Good
source of vitamin C

blood oranges with red onions, black olives and fennel dressing

serves 4
preparation time: 20 minutes

one average-size orange will generally supply an adult's daily vitamin C requirement. If you can find blood oranges, you will not be disappointed—they look amazing and taste sweet and juicy. If they are not available, choose the juiciest possible large oranges.

2 red onions, thinly sliced
approx. ¾ cup (5½ ozs.) black olives, pitted
4 blood oranges

for the fennel dressing
1 fennel bulb
juice of 1 lemon
3 tablespoons extra virgin olive oil
sea salt and freshly ground black pepper

❖ Put the red onions and olives in a bowl.
❖ Peel the oranges, working around the fruit with a sharp knife. Then cut the segments of flesh away from the membrane. Put the flesh in the bowl with the red onions and olives. Repeat with the remaining oranges.
❖ To make the fennel dressing: Trim the tough stalks off the fennel bulb, shave off the base and remove any damaged outer layers. Slice the bulb in half lengthwise, cut out the core and slice each half into thin strips. Combine the lemon juice and olive oil, season to taste with salt and pepper and mix with the fennel slices.
❖ Toss the orange segments, onions and olives lightly together. Drizzle the fennel dressing over them, and serve.

each serving contains:
Calories 185 • Protein 3g • Fat 12g (saturated 2g) • Carbohydrates 17g • Fiber 5g • Calories from fat 58% • Excellent source of vitamin C

potatoes with broad beans and mint vinaigrette

serves 4
preparation time: 10 minutes
cooking time: about 15 minutes

whenever

you make potato salad, add the dressing to the warm vegetables, and let them cool. The juicy dressing will soak into the hot potatoes so that every bite oozes with flavor.

2 lbs. new potatoes, unpeeled
¾ cup (5½ ozs.) broad beans, shelled

for the mint vinaigrette
2 large handfuls of fresh mint leaves
4 tablespoons extra virgin olive oil
juice of 1 lemon
1 tablespoon coarse-grain mustard
pinch of turbinado sugar
sea salt and freshly ground black pepper

to serve
4 spring onions, thinly sliced diagonally
handful of fresh mint leaves

❖ Put the potatoes in boiling water, and simmer for about 15 minutes, until almost cooked. They should be just tender when pierced with the point of a knife. Add the beans, and simmer for an additional 5 minutes, until the potatoes are cooked and the beans are just tender. Drain, and place in a serving dish.

❖ While the vegetables are cooking, make the mint vinaigrette: Put the mint and olive oil in a food processor or blender. Add the lemon juice, mustard and sugar, and season to taste with salt and pepper. Process until blended.

❖ Drizzle the vinaigrette over the warm potatoes and beans, and toss gently so that the vegetables are well coated. Let cool. Scatter the spring onions and fresh mint leaves over the salad, and serve.

each serving contains:
Calories 300 • Protein 7g • Fat 12g (saturated 1.5g) • Carbohydrates 42g • Fiber 5.5g • Calories from fat 37% • Good source of folic acid and vitamins B_1, B_6, and C

avocado with beans and cilantro

serves 4
preparation time: 15 minutes

I generally remove the skins from tomatoes unless the fruit is very ripe. Crisp tortilla chips work really well as a contrast to the softness of the avocado and tomatoes in this little starter.

1 cup (7 ozs.) vine-ripened tomatoes
2 cups (14½ ozs.) canned cannellini beans, drained
approx. ¾ cup (7 ozs.) can corn drained
1 red chili pepper, seeded and sliced
juice of ½ lime
1 avocado
7 tablespoons (3½ ozs.) plain corn tortilla chips
2 tablespoons extra virgin olive oil
handful of cilantro, roughly chopped

❖ Put the tomatoes in a bowl, and cover with boiling water. After 20 seconds in the boiling water, plunge them straight into cold water. Drain and skin the tomatoes, and remove their seeds with a teaspoon. Roughly chop the flesh.

❖ Put the chopped tomato, beans, corn, chili pepper and lime juice in a large bowl. Slice the avocado in half lengthwise, and remove the stone. Peel the avocado, then chop the flesh into little chunks. Add it to the beans and tomato.

❖ Arrange the tortilla chips in a single layer on a serving dish. Pile the avocado mixture and beans on top, and drizzle the olive oil over it. Scatter the cilantro leaves over the salad, and serve.

each serving contains:
Calories 410 • Protein 11g • Fat 20g (saturated 3.5g) •
Carbohydrates 48g • Fiber 10g • Calories from fat 44% • Good
source of vitamins C and E

roasted apple, onion
and sweet potato soup

serves 4
preparation time: 20 minutes
cooking time: 50 minutes

despite their name, sweet potatoes are not related to potatoes. However, they will do most things that potatoes do. You can roast, bake or mash them, and they are a great thickener for soups. They have their own natural sweetness, which is why I have added a few tart apples to help balance the flavors. They seem to enjoy being mixed with flavors such as ginger, chili, lime and coriander, as well as the fennel and cumin used here. You could always add a few parsnips to the roasting dish if they are in season—and sweet potatoes work really well with other root vegetables.

1½ teaspoons fennel seeds
1 teaspoon cumin seeds
1 lb. baby onions, quartered
3 large sweet potatoes, peeled and roughly chopped
3 apples, preferably a tart variety such as Granny Smith
3 tablespoons olive oil
3 cups (1½ pints) vegetable stock
sea salt and freshly ground black pepper
handful of fresh tarragon leaves

❖ Preheat the oven to 450°F. Dry-fry the fennel and cumin seeds in a heavy frying pan over moderate heat, turning or stirring frequently, for 3 minutes or until they start to go brown and pop. Coarsely crush the seeds using a pestle and mortar.
❖ Put the onions and sweet potatoes into a roasting dish. Core and roughly chop 2 apples, and add them to the dish. Sprinkle the crushed seeds over the vegetables and apples, and season. Drizzle 2 tablespoons olive oil over the top. Roast for 25 minutes, then turn the vegetables over and roast for an additional 25 minutes. The onions should be tender when pierced with a knife. Remove 2 potato chunks and 8 onion quarters, and set them aside.
❖ Put half the remaining vegetables into a food processor with half the stock, and process to a smooth puree. Transfer to a saucepan. Repeat with the remaining vegetables and stock. Warm the soup through over a gentle heat.
❖ Core and roughly chop the reserved apple. Roughly chop the 2 reserved potato chunks and the 8 reserved onion quarters. Heat the remaining oil in a frying pan, add the chopped apple and sauté for 5 minutes, or

until golden. Add the chopped potatoes and onions and warm through, stirring every now and then, over low heat. Season with salt and pepper to taste.

❖ When the soup is warm, divide it among four warm bowls, and spoon a little of the chopped onion, potato and apple mixture into the center of each bowl. Scatter the fresh tarragon leaves over the soup, and serve.

each serving contains:
Calories 340 • Protein 5g • Fat 9g (saturated 1.5g) • Carbohydrates 64g • Fiber 8g • Calories from fat 25% • Excellent source of vitamins A and E • Good source of vitamins B_1 and C

thai pumpkin
and coconut soup

serves 4
preparation time: 15 minutes
cooking time: 40 minutes

I have eaten something similar to this soup in a variety of restaurants, and it always tastes good. If pumpkins are not in season, use the same quantity of sweet potatoes—they love lively ingredients such as chilies, soy sauce and coconut milk. Coconut cream is one of those magical ingredients that can add a really intense creaminess to many dishes. You can find canned or frozen coconut cream in some super-markets and Asian grocery stores.

¾ cup (6 ozs.) rice noodles
1½ lb. pumpkin, peeled and cut into bite-size chunks
4 tablespoons olive oil
sea salt and freshly ground black pepper
½ teaspoon dried chili flakes
1¾ cups (14 ozs.) canned unsweetened coconut milk
½ cup (2½ ozs.) coconut cream
15 fl. ozs. vegetable stock (see page 62)
2 tablespoons light soy sauce
2 teaspoons light brown sugar, softened
1 cup (2½ ozs.) bean sprouts
5 tablespoons (2½ ozs.) carrots, cut into thin strips
large handful of cilantro, roughly chopped

❖ Preheat the oven to 425°F. Prepare the rice noodles according to the packet instructions. Put the pumpkin chunks into a roasting dish, and drizzle 2 tablespoons olive oil over it. Season with salt and pepper. Roast for 40 minutes, or until tender.

❖ While the pumpkin is roasting, heat the remaining oil in a frying pan. Add the chili flakes, and sauté them over moderate heat for about 2 minutes. Add the coconut milk, coconut cream and vegetable stock, and simmer gently, stirring, until the cream has dissolved. Stir in the soy sauce and sugar. Season well with salt and pepper. Mix in the bean sprouts and carrots, and simmer for an additional 1 minute. Add the rice noo-dles, and warm them through.

❖ Divide the chunks of pumpkin among four warm serv-ing bowls, and pour the soup over them. Scatter lots of cilantro over the top, and serve.

each serving contains:
Calories 445 • Protein 5g • Fat 26g (sat-urated 14g) • Carbohydrates 44g • Fiber 2.5g • Calories from fat 52% • Good source of vitamins A and C

creamy carrot and ginger soup with curly toasts

serves 4
preparation time: 15 minutes
cooking time: 35 minutes

for most of us, soup means breaking bread and sharing, which may be why I always tend to make soup if there are friends or family coming for lunch or supper. This soup is rich and tasty without using lots of fat. I want everyone to feel good about eating it and asking for seconds without feeling guilty.

each serving contains:
Calories 250 • Protein 7g • Fat 3g (saturated 0.5g) • Carbohydrates 48g • Fiber 14g • Calories from fat 13% • Excellent source of vitamin A • Good source of folic acid and vitamins C and E

4 teaspoons cumin seeds
5 lbs. carrots, diced
1″ piece of fresh ginger, peeled and sliced
4 slices day-old soft grain bread
sea salt and freshly ground black pepper
handful of cilantro, roughly chopped

❖ Preheat the oven to 350°F. Dry-fry the cumin seeds in a heavy frying pan over moderate heat, turning or stirring frequently, for 5 minutes or until golden. Coarsely crush the seeds using a pestle and mortar. Put the carrots, ginger and half the cumin in a large saucepan, and pour in enough water to just cover the carrots. Simmer, covered, for 30 minutes or until the carrots are soft.

❖ While the carrots are cooking, toast the slices of bread lightly on both sides. Cut off the crusts, and cut each slice in half horizontally. Carefully scrape off any doughy bits, then cut each half-slice into 2 squares and then 4 triangles. Arrange the triangles on a baking tray, and bake for 10 minutes, until golden and curly. Set aside.

❖ Drain the carrots over a bowl, and reserve the cooking liquid. Put the carrots and $3\frac{1}{2}$ fl. ozs. of the reserved liquid in a food processor, and process to a smooth puree. If the soup is too thick, add more cooking liquid.

❖ Rinse out the saucepan, return the soup and warm it through over a gentle heat. Season with salt, pepper and as much of the remaining cumin as you wish. Divide the soup among four coffee cups, scatter the cilantro over the top and pop the curly toasts on the saucers to serve.

tomato soup
with cilantro salsa

serves 4
preparation time: 20 minutes
cooking time: 20 minutes

I often turn this into a sorbet and serve it as a starter or between courses. Remember always to skin the tomatoes, or you will end up with tough bits of skin in an otherwise smooth soup.

2 lbs. ripe tomatoes
1 tablespoon olive oil
1 large onion, finely sliced
2 garlic cloves, crushed
1 teaspoon lime juice
14 fl. ozs. water
pinch of light brown sugar, softened
handful of cilantro
zest of 1 lime
sea salt and freshly ground black pepper

❖ Skin the tomatoes (see page 46), and dice the flesh.
❖ Heat the oil in a large saucepan. Fry the onion and garlic over low heat, stirring, for 10 minutes, until the onion is cooked but not brown. Reserve 2 tablespoons of the tomato flesh, and add the remainder to the saucepan. Cook gently for 10 minutes. Add the lime juice, 14 fl. ozs. water, and the sugar. Bring to a boil, then reduce the heat, and simmer for 5 minutes. Let cool slightly.
❖ Put the soup in a food processor, and process to a smooth puree. Pass the puree through a sieve into a clean saucepan, and season to taste. Add half the cilantro, and warm the soup through over a gentle heat.
❖ Divide the soup among four warm serving bowls. Mix the reserved diced tomato, the remaining cilantro and the lime zest together, and put a spoonful of the salsa in the middle of each bowl. Serve.

For a tomato sorbet

❖ Let the puree sit until it is cold, then add a couple of dashes of Tabasco sauce. Either process the puree in an ice cream machine, following the manufacturer's instructions, or pour it into a freezeproof container and freeze it for 3 hours. Take it out of the freezer every hour, mash it with a fork, and return it to the freezer. Add a little drizzle of vodka over the top, and serve with celery sticks, or with the cilantro salsa.

each serving contains:
Calories 75 • Protein 2g • Fat 3g (saturated 0.6g) • Carbohydrates 10g • Fiber 3g • Calories from fat 42% • Good source of vitamins C and A

corn, coconut, lime
and basil soup

serves 4
preparation time: 20 minutes
cooking time: 15 minutes, plus 1¼ hours for boiling the stock, if making

I try to make soups with ingredients that provide the flavor rather than having to rely heavily on stocks. The stock for this particular recipe is made from the corn cobs left over when the kernels have been removed. However, if fresh corn is not in season, use 14 ounces of canned corn and a good vegetable stock (see page 62) instead. Similarly, if kaffir lime leaves, which add a wonderfully subtle citrus flavor to the soup, are not available, substitute the fine zest (no pith) of half a lime. (Kaffir lime leaves are available in Asian markets.) Jalapeño chili peppers are probably the best-known chilies around. They are about 1–1½ inches long, with a full flavor and medium heat. As with most chilies, the heat is concentrated in the seeds and the membrane, which holds the seeds to the flesh.

4 ears of corn
5½ cups (2¾ pints) water
2 tablespoons vegetable oil
1″ piece of fresh ginger, peeled and grated
2 shallots, sliced
1 jalapeño chili pepper, seeded and finely chopped
3 kaffir lime leaves or zest of ½ lime
4 fl. ozs. canned unsweetened coconut milk
large handful of fresh basil leaves
2 limes, each cut into chunks

❖ Scrape the kernels from the ears with a sharp knife, and put the kernels in a bowl. Set aside.

❖ Break each of the ears into 2 or 3 pieces. Put them in a large saucepan, and add 5½ cups water. Bring to a boil, then reduce the heat and simmer, covered, for 1 hour. You will need to skim the foam from the top of the liquid with a large spoon, especially for the first 30 minutes. Strain the stock through a fine-mesh strainer or cheesecloth.

❖ Heat the oil in a large clean saucepan, and add the ginger, shallots and jalapeño. Fry gently for 5 minutes, stirring frequently, until the shallots are softened. Add the kaffir lime leaves or lime zest, reserved corn stock (or the equivalent volume of vegetable stock) and coconut milk. Bring to a boil, then reduce the heat immediately, and simmer for 5 minutes. Add water, if necessary, to achieve the texture you prefer. Add the reserved kernels, and simmer for another 5 minutes.

❖ Ladle the soup into warm bowls. Stack about 6 basil leaves together, roll them into a cigar shape and slice thinly. Repeat with the remaining basil. Scatter the basil strips over the soup. Serve with wedges of lime.

each serving contains:
Calories 210 • Protein 5g • Fat 11g (saturated 3.6g) •
Carbohydrates 23g • Fiber 2.6g • Calories from fat 48%

wild mushroom soup

serves 4
preparation time: 15 minutes
cooking time: 10 minutes

I tend not to use a lot of tofu in my vegan cooking, but this soup is perfect for it. The flavors from the mushrooms and harissa soak into the cubes of bean curd, adding texture and flavor to the finished dish. You can replace the vegetable stock with the same quantity of stock made with Swiss vegetable vegan bouillon powder. If you can find toasted sesame oil, use it instead of the plain version when you serve the soup. (Harissa is available in Middle Eastern grocery stores.)

3 cups (8 ozs.) fresh oyster mushrooms
2 cups (5½ ozs.) shiitake mushrooms
2 tablespoons vegetable oil
2 garlic cloves, crushed
2" piece of fresh ginger, peeled and grated
¾ cup (7 ozs.) canned straw mushrooms, drained
2 tablespoons sake
3 cups (1½ pints) vegetable stock (see page 62)
2 tablespoons corn flour
2 tablespoons warm water
1 cup (4½ ozs.) firm tofu, diced
sea salt and freshly ground black pepper

to serve
2 tablespoons sesame oil
3 tablespoons sesame seeds

❖ Remove and discard the stalks of the oyster and shiitake mushrooms. Slice each mushroom in half.
❖ Heat the oil in a large saucepan. Add the garlic, ginger, sliced mushrooms and straw mushrooms. Sauté over moderate heat for 5 minutes, or until the garlic and ginger are softened. Add the sake and stock, and bring to a boil. Reduce the heat to a simmer.
❖ In a small bowl, mix the corn flour with 2 tablespoons warm water to form a smooth paste. Stir the paste into the soup. Continue stirring; the soup will thicken quite quickly. When the soup has thickened, add the tofu, and season to taste with salt and pepper.
❖ Divide the soup among four warm bowls. Drizzle a little sesame oil over each serving, and scatter a few sesame seeds on top. Serve.

each serving contains:
Calories 205 • Protein 8g • Fat 15g (saturated 2g) • Carbohydrates 8g • Fiber 2g • Calories from fat 69%

roasted squash soup
with fresh cilantro

serves 4
preparation time: 15 minutes
cooking time: 1 1/2 hours

this is a soup for winter, when butternut squash is readily available in markets and supermarkets. It is quick to prepare—the only time-consuming part is roasting the squash, but at least you can put them in the oven and do something else while they merrily cook away. Squash have a chameleon quality and are just as at home in a sweet tart (see Pecan and Butternut Squash Tart, page 204) as they are in a soup. Although the addition of vanilla is optional, I find that it rounds all the flavors off perfectly.

1 large butternut squash, about 4 cups (2 lbs.)
4 tablespoons olive oil
2 shallots, sliced
pinch of grated fresh nutmeg
1 cinnamon stick
big pinch of saffron threads
2 cups (1 pint) water
2 drops of vanilla extract (optional)
sea salt and freshly ground black pepper
large handful of cilantro, roughly chopped

❖ Preheat the oven to 400°F. Rub the squash with 2 tablespoons oil, then put it in a shallow roasting tin, and bake for 1 hour. Let cool slightly.

❖ Slice the squash in half, scoop out the seeds with a teaspoon and remove the peel. Put the pulp into a bowl, and mash it well.

❖ Heat the remaining oil in a large saucepan. Add the shallots, nutmeg, cinnamon and saffron, and fry over moderate heat, stirring, for 5 minutes, until the shallots are softened. Add the squash and sauté, stirring, for 2 minutes. Pour the water into the saucepan, bring to a boil, then reduce the heat. Add the vanilla extract, if using, and season with salt and pepper. Cover, and simmer for 30 minutes. Add more water, if necessary, to achieve the texture you prefer.

❖ Put the soup in a food processor, and process to a smooth puree. Divide the soup among four warm bowls, scatter fresh cilantro over the top and serve.

each serving contains:
Calories 185 • Protein 2.5g • Fat 11g (saturated 1.5g) •
Carbohydrates 19.5g • Fiber 3.5g • Calories from fat 55% •
Excellent source of vitamins A and C • Good source of vitamin E

spicy gazpacho soup
with paprika croutons

serves 4
preparation time: 20 minutes
cooking time: 30 minutes

traditional

gazpacho is served cold. This warm version is delicious topped with hot paprika croutons. Serve a little bowl of the croutons with the soup. If you are short of time, just make the gazpacho—which is incredibly quick—and serve it with fresh bread.

2 lbs. very ripe cherry tomatoes or baby plum tomatoes
1 cucumber, peeled and seeded
1 garlic clove, chopped
1 red chili pepper, seeded and finely chopped
3 spring onions, finely chopped
4 tablespoons extra virgin olive oil
1 tablespoon red wine vinegar
2 teaspoons turbinado sugar
small handful of fresh arugula
pinch of cayenne pepper
sea salt

for the croutons
4 slices white bread or ciabatta, about 1″ thick
4–5 tablespoons extra virgin olive oil
large pinch of sea salt
large pinch of paprika

to serve
pinch of cayenne pepper
handful of roughly torn fresh arugula

❖ To make the croutons: Preheat the oven to 375°F. Cut the bread into 1″ cubes, and place cubes in a bowl. Add the olive oil, salt and paprika, and toss to coat the cubes. Place the cubes on a baking tray in a single layer. Bake for about 20 minutes, turning once, until the croutons are golden and crispy on the outside but still moist in the middle.

❖ Put all the soup ingredients except the cayenne pepper and salt into a food processor, and process to a smooth puree. Pour the soup into a saucepan, and heat gently for 5–10 minutes, or until warm. Season to taste.

❖ Divide the soup among four warm bowls. Top with a few croutons, and sprinkle a little cayenne and scatter some torn arugula over each serving. Serve immediately, with the remaining croutons in a small bowl.

each serving contains:
Calories 340 • Protein 5g • Fat 23g (saturated 3g) • Carbohydrates 29g • Fiber 3.5g • Calories from fat 62% • Excellent source of vitamin C • Good source of vitamins A and E

vegetable stock

makes approx. 2 quarts
preparation time: 20 minutes
cooking time: 1 1/4 hours

if you want to make stock for soups, this is for you. As with all recipes, the finished product will only be as good as its raw ingredients, so don't be tempted to use old vegetables that lack flavor. Freeze any stock you don't use immediately.

2 tablespoons olive oil
3 medium-size onions, roughly chopped
4 carrots, roughly chopped
2 leeks, roughly chopped
1 celery stick, roughly chopped
1 small green lettuce
1/2 head of broccoli, cut into florets
1 bay leaf
4 black peppercorns
pinch of sea salt
handful of fresh flat-leaf parsley, roughly chopped
12 cups (6 pints) water

❖ Heat the olive oil in a large saucepan. Add the onions, carrots, leeks, celery, lettuce and broccoli, and sweat the vegetables over low heat for 20 minutes. Add the bay leaf, peppercorns, salt, parsley and water. Bring to a boil, then reduce the heat and simmer, partially covered, for 1 1/4 hours over very low heat—it is important that the liquid only just bubbles. Every now and then you will need to skim the foam from the top of the liquid with a large spoon.

❖ Strain the stock, making sure you don't push any of the vegetables through the sieve.

❖ Let cool, and refrigerate (or freeze) until needed.

each serving contains:
No significant nutrients

snacks & light meals

moroccan spiced couscous
with fruit

serves 4
preparation time: 15 minutes, plus standing time
cooking time: 20 minutes

I have a real passion for couscous, one of the truly great dishes of Morocco, Tunisia and Algeria. Couscous is made from strong or hard wheat, which is moistened with water and coated with a fine flour, then rolled into tiny, cream-colored pellets. Like other carbohydrates, couscous relies on the ingredients that you add to it for flavor and contrasting texture.

1 lb. couscous
8½ fl. ozs. vegetable stock
pinch of saffron threads
½ cup (2 ozs.) dried apricots, roughly chopped
¼ cup (2 ozs.) dates, pitted and roughly chopped
⅓ cup (2 ozs.) raisins
sea salt and freshly ground black pepper
pinch of chili powder, preferably Kashmiri chili powder
2 tablespoons lemon oil or olive oil
juice of 1 lemon
2 cups (14½ ozs.) canned chickpeas, drained and rinsed
handful of fresh mint leaves, roughly chopped
handful of cilantro, roughly chopped
¾ cup (2½ ozs.) flaked almonds

❖ Preheat the oven to 400°F. Put the couscous in an ovenproof dish. Mix the stock, saffron, apricots, dates and raisins in a saucepan, and bring to a boil. Pour the hot stock and fruit over the couscous. Add just enough boiling water to cover the grains, but do not flood them. Set aside for 15 minutes.

❖ Fluff up the couscous with a fork, and season it with salt, pepper and chili powder to taste. Drizzle the lemon or olive oil and lemon juice over it, and add the chickpeas. Mix the ingredients well, then cover the dish.

❖ Bake the couscous for 15 minutes. Fluff up the grains, and stir in the mint and cilantro. Return the couscous to the oven for an additional 5 minutes. Meanwhile, dry-fry the almonds in a heavy frying pan over moderate heat, turning or stirring frequently, for 5 minutes until they are golden. Scatter the almonds over the couscous, and serve immediately.

each serving contains:
Calories 630 • Protein 20g • Fat 20g (saturated 2g) •
Carbohydrates 98g • Fiber 7g • Calories from fat 29% • Excellent
source of vitamins B$_1$, B$_3$ (niacin), B$_6$ and E, and also iron

griddled red onion slices
with couscous

serves 4
preparation time: 10 minutes, plus 30 minutes standing time
cooking time: about 20 minutes

red onions cook really well on a griddle—they go soft in the middle and char on the edges. If you have slightly more time, parboil the onions before griddling them. The texture and flavor will be slightly different, but equally delicious. Leave the couscous to stand, covered, in a warm place for as long as possible after pouring warm water or vegetable stock (see page 62) over it. It will be much lighter and fluffier as a result. There are many ways of preparing couscous, but this one is my favorite.

1 lb. couscous
4 red onions
olive oil, for griddling
juice of ½ lime
sea salt and freshly ground black pepper

to serve
large handful of fresh flat-leaf parsley, roughly chopped
1 lime, cut into 4 wedges

❖ Put the couscous in a bowl, and add just enough warm water or vegetable stock to cover the grains, but do not flood them. Cover, and let sit for at least 30 minutes in a warm place.
❖ Cut the onions vertically into ½″ slices. Brush a griddle with a little olive oil, and heat until very hot. Cook the onion slices for about 3–4 minutes on each side—you may need to do this in 2 batches. If you do not have a griddle pan, heat a grill until it is very hot, and grill the onions for the same amount of time.
❖ Fluff up the grains of couscous with a fork. Squeeze the lime juice over them, and season well with salt and pepper. Divide the couscous among four warm plates. Arrange the onion slices on top of the couscous, and scatter fresh parsley over the top. Serve with the lime wedges.

each serving contains:
Calories 310 • Protein 7.5g • Fat 4g (saturated 0.4g) • Carbohydrates 65g • Fiber 1g • Calories from fat 12% • Good source of iron

warm couscous with garlic, black olives and tomatoes

serves 4
preparation time: 15 minutes, plus 30 minutes standing time
cooking time: 5 minutes

I adore the combination of garlic, olives and tomatoes—it whisks me off to a Mediterranean country every time I eat it. The good news is that 10 large olives contain about one-fifth of an adult's daily iron requirement.

3 tablespoons extra virgin olive oil
1 garlic clove, crushed
1 lb. couscous
8 medium-size vine-ripened plum tomatoes; choose juicy, ripe ones
approx. ¾ cup (7 ozs.) black olives, pitted
juice of ½ lemon
handful of fresh flat-leaf parsley, roughly chopped
sea salt and freshly ground black pepper

❖ Heat the olive oil in a saucepan, add the garlic, and fry gently for 5 minutes, or until it is softened but not brown. Add the couscous, and stir until well coated. Remove the saucepan from the heat, and add just enough warm water to cover the grains, but do not flood them. Cover, and let sit for at least 30 minutes in a warm place.

❖ Put the tomatoes in a bowl, and cover with boiling water. After 20 seconds in the boiling water, plunge them straight into cold water. Drain and skin the tomatoes, then dice their flesh. Roughly chop the olives.

❖ Fluff up the grains of couscous with a fork, and squeeze the lemon juice over them. Add the tomatoes, olives and half of the parsley. Mix together. Season with salt and pepper. Divide among four warm plates, scatter the remaining parsley over the top and serve.

each serving contains:
Calories 380 • Protein 8g • Fat 12g (saturated 2g) • Carbohydrates 62g • Fiber 3g • Calories from fat 30% • Excellent source of vitamin C • Good source of iron and vitamin E

bright red pepper pesto linguine

serves 4
preparation time: 20 minutes
cooking time: 10–12 minutes

the color and flavor of this sauce is brilliant and intense. I developed the recipe while roasting peppers for a soup. There were some left over, so I tossed them in a food processor with a few other ingredients. Always wash your hands immediately after preparing fresh chilies, and be careful not to rub your eyes—you'll be in agony.

4 red peppers
2 red chili peppers
¼ cup (2½ ozs.) hazelnuts
large handful of fresh basil leaves
2 garlic cloves, crushed
3 tablespoons extra virgin olive oil, plus extra for tossing
12 ozs. linguine
sea salt and freshly ground black pepper
handful of fresh basil leaves, roughly torn

❖ Preheat grill or broiler to high. Put the red peppers and chili peppers under the flame source, and cook, turning until they are black and charred all over. Put them immediately into a plastic bag. Seal and let sit for 5 minutes—the steam will help to loosen the pepper and chili skins.

❖ Peel the peppers and chilies, and remove their seeds with a teaspoon. Dry-fry the hazelnuts in a heavy frying pan over moderate heat, turning or stirring frequently, for 5 minutes or until golden. Allow the nuts to cool a little, then chop them roughly. Put the basil, garlic and chopped hazelnuts in a food processor, and process to a coarse paste. With the motor running, gradually add the olive oil. Add the flesh of the peppers and chilies, and process again until the pesto sauce is smooth.

❖ Bring a large saucepan of water to a boil, and cook the linguine according to the instructions on the packet. Drain, return the linguine to the saucepan and add the pesto and a little olive oil. Toss well, and season with salt and pepper. Scatter fresh basil over the top, and serve.

each serving contains:
Calories 575 • Protein 15g • Fat 23g
(saturated 2.5g) • Carbohydrates 82g •
Fiber 8g • Calories from fat 35% •
Excellent source of vitamins A, C and E

fresh ginger and basil pasta

serves 4
preparation time: 10 minutes
cooking time: 10 minutes, depending on the type of pasta

one of the great advantages of vegan cooking is that the flavors of fresh herbs and roots such as garlic and ginger are not masked by dairy products. They remain clean, crisp and fresh. Wherever and whenever possible, I eat garlic and ginger in their most effective state: raw. Garlic is especially good for improving the body's immune system.

1 tablespoon peeled, roughly chopped fresh ginger
1 tablespoon cilantro
3 tablespoons fresh basil leaves
2 tablespoons finely chopped garlic
1 tablespoon peanut oil
2 teaspoons sesame oil
sea salt and freshly ground black pepper
12 ozs. pasta of your choice
handful of fresh basil leaves, roughly torn

❖ Put the ginger, cilantro, basil, garlic and peanut and sesame oils in a food processor, and process until smooth. Season with salt and pepper. Set the sauce aside.
❖ Bring a large saucepan of water to a boil, and cook the pasta according to the instructions on the packet. Drain, return the pasta to the saucepan, and add the sauce. Toss well. Scatter fresh basil over the top, and serve.

each serving contains:
Calories 335 • Protein 10g • Fat 6g (saturated 1g) • Carbohydrates 64g • Fiber 2.5g • Calories from fat 16%

summer pasta salad

serves 4
preparation time: 15 minutes
cooking time: 10–12 minutes

this may seem very simple, but I expect that many of you will love it and cook it over and over again. I love meals like this one, especially when time is short and I need a recipe that happily accepts any fresh vegetables that happen to be in the fridge. Add the dressing to the hot pasta so that it absorbs the fresh mint and lemon flavors.

12 ozs. spiral pasta
1 cup (3½ ozs.) baby corn, halved lengthwise
1 cup (3½ ozs.) sugar snap peas, halved lengthwise
½ cucumber, unpeeled
½ cup (4 ozs.) black olives, pitted
6 medium-size vine-ripened tomatoes, quartered; choose ripe, juicy ones
sea salt and freshly ground black pepper
handful of fresh mint leaves, roughly chopped

for the dressing
4 tablespoons olive oil
juice of 1 lemon
2 tablespoons fresh mint leaves, roughly chopped
sea salt and freshly ground black pepper

❖ To make the dressing: Put all the ingredients in a screw-top jar, and shake vigorously until well blended. Set aside.
❖ Bring a large saucepan of water to a boil, and cook the pasta according to the instructions on the packet. Drain, and place in a warm serving dish.
❖ Meanwhile, bring a small saucepan of water to a boil. Add the baby corn and sugar snap peas, and blanch for 2 minutes. Drain, and add to the pasta. Add the dressing to the hot pasta, and toss until it is well coated.

❖ Cut the cucumber in half lengthwise, and scoop out the seeds with a teaspoon. Cut the cucumber into very thin strips using a vegetable peeler. Add the cucumber, olives and tomatoes to the pasta. Toss well to mix. Divide the pasta among four warm plates, and season with salt and pepper. Scatter fresh mint over the top, and serve.

each serving contains:
Calories 480 • Protein 13g • Fat 16g (saturated 2.5g) •
Carbohydrates 74g • Fiber 6g • Calories from fat 31% • Excellent
source of vitamin C

roast vine tomatoes
and pasta

serves 4
preparation time: 20 minutes
cooking time: 30 minutes

roasting

tomatoes with a little citrus juice gives them a completely new identity. This recipe is for a pasta dish, but the tomatoes are just as successful squashed on to slices of hot toast and served as a starter.

2 tablespoons olive oil
6 small pickling onions, peeled
2 teaspoons soft light brown sugar
1¼ cups (10 ozs.) vine-ripened baby plum tomatoes or cherry tomatoes, quartered
juice of ½ lime
12 ozs. pasta of your choice
sea salt and freshly ground black pepper

❖ Preheat the oven to 425°F. Heat the oil in a frying pan, and fry the onions over moderate heat for about 5 minutes, until they start to brown. Sprinkle the sugar over the onions, and fry for another 10 minutes. Let cool a little, then cut the onions in half. Transfer them to a shallow ovenproof dish. Place the tomatoes on top, and drizzle the lime juice over them. Roast in the oven for 15 minutes.

❖ Bring a large saucepan of water to a boil, and cook the pasta according to the instructions on the packet. Drain, return the pasta to the saucepan, and add the sauce. Toss well, and season with salt and pepper. Serve immediately.

each serving contains:
Calories 375 • Protein 11g • Fat 7g (saturated 3g) • Carbohydrates 70g • Fiber 6g • Calories from fat 17% • Excellent source of vitamins A and C

rich mushroom sauce
with tagliatelle

serves 4
preparation time: 20 minutes, plus soaking time
cooking time: 30 minutes

this is a quick pasta dish, provided you remember to soak the porcini beforehand. It is quite exciting watching the dried mushrooms come back to life as they absorb the water. If you ever use them in a recipe that does not require the soaking liquor, pour it into ice cube trays and freeze it—it is too good to be wasted. You can use a couple of cubes in soups or sauces to add a quick burst of flavor.

½ cup (½ oz.) dried porcini mushrooms
10 fl. ozs. boiling water
1 tablespoon olive oil
½ medium-size onion, finely chopped
1 garlic clove, crushed
1¼ lbs. portobello or brown mushrooms, finely chopped
1 tablespoon marsala or brandy (optional)
12 ozs. tagliatelle
handful of fresh flat-leaf parsley, roughly chopped
sea salt and freshly ground black pepper

❖ Cover the porcini with the boiling water, and let soak for 30 minutes.

❖ Heat the oil in a frying pan, and sauté the onion over moderate heat for 5 minutes, until soft and golden. Add the garlic, and sauté for 1 minute more. Drain the porcini, and reserve the soaking liquid. Chop the porcini finely. Add the porcini and portobello mushrooms to the onion. Cook over low heat for 20 minutes, then add the reserved soaking liquid and marsala or brandy, if using. Turn up the heat, and simmer for 5 minutes, or until the liquid has reduced slightly.

❖ Bring a large saucepan of water to a boil, and cook the tagliatelle according to the instructions on the packet. Drain, return the pasta to the saucepan, and add the sauce and parsley. Season with salt and pepper. Toss well, and serve.

each serving contains:
Calories 365 • Protein 14g • Fat 5g (saturated 1g) • Carbohydrates 67g • Fiber 5g • Calories from fat 3% • Good source of niacin

vivid beet and horseradish gnocchi

serves 4
preparation time: 20 minutes
cooking time: 2 hours

beets need to be handled and cooked with care—their wonderful vivid color will leach out into the water if they are boiled. In a dish like this the color is vitally important so I roast the beets with their skins on and peel them before pureeing. The result is a fabulous bright red sauce with a wonderful flavor and texture. It goes as well with pasta or polenta as it does with gnocchi.

1 lb. raw beets, unpeeled
1 red onion, chopped
sprig of fresh rosemary
sprig of fresh thyme
2 lemon quarters
1 tablespoon olive oil
sea salt and freshly ground black pepper
2″ piece of fresh horseradish root, peeled and grated
12 ozs. gnocchi
handful of fresh thyme leaves

❖ Preheat the oven to 325°F. Trim the beets, and put them in a roasting pan with the onion, herbs and lemon quarters. Drizzle the olive oil over them, and season well with salt and pepper. Cover the pan with foil, and roast for 2 hours. Let cool.

❖ Slip the skins off the beets (they should come off easily), and cut the flesh of half of them into chunks. Put the chunks in a food processor, and process to a puree. Finely chop the remaining flesh, and add it to the puree. Season to taste with salt and pepper, and add horseradish to taste. Transfer the puree to a saucepan, and warm through gently.

❖ Bring a large saucepan of water to a boil, and cook the gnocchi according to the instructions on the packet. Remove the gnocchi with a slotted spoon, and divide them among four warm plates. Top with the beet sauce. Scatter thyme leaves over each serving, and serve.

each serving contains:
Calories 215 • Protein 5g • Fat 3g (saturated 0.5g) • Carbohydrates 40g • Fiber 2.5g • Calories from fat 14% • Good source of folic acid

puree of beans and potatoes with olive oil

serves 4
preparation time: 10 minutes
cooking time: 20 minutes

If you have ever been to Nimes in Provence, there is a strong chance you will be familiar with this dish. It is a joy to eat—both comforting and delicious—and very simple to make. Serve it with a few fresh green vegetables as a main course. Once again, I have snuck in some raw garlic—it is *so* good for you.

2 cups (15 ozs.) canned cannellini beans, drained
2 medium-size potatoes, peeled and cut into chunks
1 bay leaf
2 tablespoons olive oil
1 medium-size onion, sliced
3 garlic cloves, crushed
juice of ½ lemon
pinch of cayenne pepper

❖ Coarsely mash the beans in a bowl. Bring a saucepan of water to a boil, add the potato chunks and bay leaf, and simmer for about 15 minutes, until the potatoes are tender. Drain, discard the bay leaf, and return the saucepan to the heat. Dry the potatoes over very low heat, shaking gently, then mash them.

❖ While the potato is boiling, heat the olive oil in a frying pan, and fry the onion and 2 crushed garlic cloves for 2 minutes. Add the mashed beans and mashed potatoes and mix to a puree. Warm the puree through over low heat, stirring every now and then to make sure it doesn't stick to the pan.

❖ Remove the puree from the heat and beat in the remaining crushed garlic and the lemon juice. Season to taste with cayenne pepper, and serve immediately.

each serving contains:
Calories 215 • Protein 11g • Fat 6g (saturated 0.9g) •
Carbohydrates 30g • Fiber 7g • Calories from fat 27%

samosas with mango chutney

serves 4
preparation time: 20 minutes
cooking time: about 35 minutes

filo pastry is great to cook with because of its light, crisp texture. However, it is incredibly thin and consequently will dry out if exposed to the air. The trick is to keep the sheets covered with a clean damp cloth until you are ready to use them.

2 medium-size ripe tomatoes
2 teaspoons cumin seeds
1 teaspoon coriander seeds
1 lb. potatoes, peeled
2 tablespoons vegetable oil
2 large onions, sliced
2 green chili peppers, seeded and finely sliced
2 garlic cloves, crushed
¼ cup (1¾ ozs.) peas
handful of cilantro, finely chopped
handful of fresh mint leaves, finely chopped
4 filo pastry sheets, thawed if frozen
vegetable oil, for deep-frying
mango chutney, to serve

❖ Put the tomatoes in a bowl, and cover with boiling water. After 20 seconds in the boiling water, plunge them straight into cold water. Drain and skin the tomatoes, then dice their flesh.

❖ Dry-fry the cumin and coriander seeds in a heavy frying pan over moderate heat, turning or stirring frequently, for a couple of minutes, or until they start to pop and turn golden. Crush coarsely using a pestle and mortar.

❖ Bring a saucepan of water to a boil. Add the potatoes, and simmer for about 15 minutes, until tender. Drain the potatoes, and chop them into small pieces.

❖ While the potatoes are boiling, heat the oil in a frying pan. Fry the onions, chili peppers and garlic over moderate heat for 5 minutes, until the onions are soft and golden. Add the crushed cumin and coriander, and fry for another 2 minutes. Add the tomatoes, peas, potatoes, chopped cilantro and mint, and fry for an additional 2 minutes. Remove the filling from the heat, and let cool.

❖ Cut a sheet of filo pastry in half horizontally. Cover the other 3 sheets and the remaining half with a clean, damp cloth. Put 1 tablespoon of the filling in the center of the right-hand side of the half-sheet. Bring one corner of the sheet over the filling, then roll the pastry and filling over twice to make a triangle. Seal the edges with a little water. Repeat with the remaining filo pastry and filling to make a total of 8 samosas.

❖ Half-fill a deep fryer or a deep, heavy saucepan with the vegetable oil, and heat to 350°F. To test the temperature, drop a cube of bread in the oil—it should brown within 2 minutes. Drop 2 samosas into the oil, and deep fry for 5–7 minutes, until golden brown. Drain on paper towels. Repeat with the remaining samosas. Serve the samosas with a bowl of mango chutney as an accompaniment.

each serving contains:
Calories 200 • Protein 5g • Fat 6.5g (saturated 0.5g) • Carbohydrates 31g • Fiber 3g • Calories from fat 30%

mediterranean galette

serves 4
preparation time: 20 minutes
cooking time: 20 minutes

baking the pastry before adding the topping ensures that you have a crisp, light base underneath the soft vegetables. Tapenade is a spicy paste made from olives and capers that adds lots of flavor, as well as acting as a barrier between the pastry and vegetables. It is available at larger supermarkets. Note: You may need to combine one sheet of puff pastry with some of another to get the 13 ounces specified in this recipe.

approx. 1¾ cups (13 ozs.) sheet puff pastry, thawed if frozen
2 tablespoons olive oil
1 red onion, sliced
1 zucchini, finely sliced
1 red pepper, seeded and finely sliced
2 portobello mushrooms, thinly sliced
sea salt and freshly ground black pepper
2 tablespoons tapenade
handful of fresh basil leaves, roughly torn

❖ Preheat the oven to 400°F. Use an upturned plate or flan pan to cut an 8″ circle of pastry, then prick the whole surface evenly with a fork. Heat a baking sheet in the oven for 2–3 minutes. Scatter a few drops of water over the hot baking sheet, and put the pastry circle on top. Bake for 10–15 minutes, until golden and puffy. The drops of water will turn to steam in the hot oven and help the pastry to rise. Turn the pastry over, and return it to the oven for 5 minutes.

❖ Meanwhile, heat the oil in a frying pan. Add the onion, zucchini and red pepper, and fry over moderate heat for 10 minutes, until the vegetables have softened. Add the mushrooms, season well with salt and pepper, and sauté for another 5 minutes.

❖ Spread the tapenade over the pastry base, spoon the vegetables over it, and return the galette to the oven for 5 minutes. Scatter fresh basil over the top, and serve warm.

each serving contains:
Calories 440 • Protein 7g • Fat 29g (saturated 19g) •
Carbohydrates 40g • Fiber 2g • Calories from fat 59% • Excellent source of vitamins A and C

fennel and ginger tarts

serves 4
preparation time: 15 minutes
cooking time: 30 minutes

make sure you roll the pastry thin so that the end result is crisp with a soft, sticky center. Remember to use pie pastry that is not derived from any animal products. (You may have some pastry left over, since this recipe calls for just 8 ounces of ready-made crust.) If you are lucky enough to find fennel bulbs that still have their feathery fronds, chop the fronds finely and scatter them over the tarts at the end of cooking. Otherwise use dill—it comes from the same family as fennel, and the taste is not dissimilar. Choose pale green young fennel bulbs. Reserve any trimmings left over after preparing the bulbs, and add them to a vegetable stock (see page 62). Serve the tarts with a green salad and chunks of fresh lemon.

8 ozs. ready-made pie pastry, thawed if frozen
5 large fennel bulbs
2 tablespoons extra virgin olive oil
1″ piece of fresh ginger, peeled and cut into thin matchsticks
sea salt and freshly ground black pepper

to serve
handful of fennel fronds, finely sliced
1 lemon, cut into chunks

❖ Preheat the oven to 350°F. Lightly grease four 4″ pastry tins. Roll out the pastry to a thickness of about $\frac{1}{2}$ inch, and cut 4 circles slightly bigger than the tins. Line the tins with the pastry, and prick the bases with a fork. Chill in the fridge for 10 minutes.
❖ Line the pastry cases with greaseproof paper and baking beans, and bake blind for 10–15 minutes, until golden and slightly crispy.
❖ Trim the tough stalks off the fennel bulbs, shave off the bases, and remove any damaged outer layers. Slice each bulb in half vertically, cut out the core, and slice the bulb into 5–7 strips. Heat the oil in a frying pan, add the ginger and fennel, and fry gently for 20 minutes, or until the fennel is soft and caramelized. Season with salt and pepper. You may have to do this in 2 batches depending on the size of the frying pan; the fennel will steam and not get brown if the pan is too small. Spoon the caramelized fennel into the pastry cases, and return to the oven for 5 minutes.
❖ Scatter the fennel fronds over the tarts. Serve warm with chunks of lemon.

each serving contains:
Calories 320 • Protein 4.5g • Fat 21g (saturated 6.5g)
Carbohydrates 29g • Fiber 4.5g • Calories from fat 60%

four-onion croustades

serves 4
preparation time: 20 minutes
cooking time: 45 minutes

I once made a five-onion tart on television, and not one member of the audience could name all of them. They were amazed to learn that chives and garlic are both members of the onion family. Since then I have experimented with soups, tarts and pizzas that contain a number of different onions. Combining them in one dish always seems to work really well, as they complement one another in flavor, color and texture. Although onions contain a lot of natural sugar, I have added a little brown sugar to speed the caramelization process along a little. The little bread cups are excellent for serving vegetables. For a sweet version, use a good fruity bread for the croustades, and dust with cinnamon and sugar before baking. Fill them with poached fruit.

8 medium slices white bread, crusts removed
sea salt and freshly ground black pepper
3 tablespoons vegetable oil
2 medium leeks
1 garlic clove, crushed
1 Spanish onion, sliced
1 tablespoon chopped chives
1 tablespoon light brown sugar, softened
handful of fresh chives, finely chopped

❖ Preheat the oven to 325°F. Lightly oil 8 tart pans. Flatten the bread slices with a rolling pin. Brush both sides of each slice with oil, and season with salt and pepper. Press the slices into the patty pans. Bake for 40 minutes, until crisp and golden.

❖ Meanwhile, chop each leek into 4 pieces, then cut each piece into long, thin strips. Heat about $1\frac{1}{2}$ tablespoons oil in a frying pan, and add the garlic, leeks, onion and chives. Sauté over moderate heat for 5 minutes, until the vegetables are softened. Add the sugar, cover, and sauté for another 10 minutes, or until the onions have caramelized. Season to taste with salt and pepper.

❖ Spoon the caramelized onions into the crispy croustades, and heat through in the oven for 5 minutes. Scatter fresh chives over the top, and serve immediately.

each serving contains:
Calories 270 • Protein 7g • Fat 9g (saturated 1g) • Carbohydrates 41g • Fiber 2.5g • Calories from fat 33%

fresh broad beans
with paprika and lemon

serves 4
preparation time: 20 minutes
cooking time: 15 minutes

broad beans appear quite frequently in Moroccan cookery, so I have chosen Moroccan flavors such as paprika and lemon for this dish. If fresh beans are not available, use frozen ones, but make sure that you cook them slightly longer. Serve on toast or with a fresh salad.

1 lb. fresh broad beans *or* frozen broad beans, thawed
1 small onion, finely chopped
3 tablespoons extra virgin olive oil
sea salt and freshly ground black pepper
2–3 tablespoons (1¾ ozs.) cilantro, roughly chopped
1 teaspoon paprika
juice of ½ lemon
zest of 1 lemon, cut into strips

❖ Shell the beans. Put them in a saucepan, add the onion and olive oil, and season with salt and pepper. Cover with water (not more than 7 fl. ozs.), bring to a boil, and simmer for 10 minutes. Add the cilantro, paprika and lemon juice and simmer, covered, for an additional 5 minutes, or until the beans are tender and the liquid is reduced.

❖ Transfer the beans to a serving dish, and garnish with the lemon zest. Serve hot, warm or at room temperature.

each serving contains:
Calories 150 • Protein 7g • Fat 9g (saturated 1g) • Carbohydrates 10g • Fiber 7g • Calories from fat 66% • Excellent source of vitamin C • Good source of folic acid

warm tomato
and eggplant stacks

serves 4
preparation time: 20 minutes
cooking time: 20 minutes

very basic recipe ideas can often be transformed into masterpieces by the way they are presented. These stacks are little towers of purple, green and red with a delicious dressing dribbling down the sides and a flourish of fresh herbs scattered over the top.

4 beefsteak tomatoes
olive oil, for cooking
1–2 small eggplants, cut into eight ½" slices
2 zucchini, cut into ½" slices
handful of fresh basil leaves, roughly torn

for the dressing
1 garlic clove
pinch of sea salt
juice and zest of 1 large lemon
6 tablespoons extra virgin olive oil
freshly ground black pepper
2 tablespoons finely chopped fresh mint leaves

❖ Preheat the oven to 375°F. Score a cross in the top of each tomato, put them in a bowl, and cover with boiling water. After 20 seconds in the boiling water, plunge them straight into cold water. Drain and skin the tomatoes, then cut each one into 4 thick slices.

❖ Brush a griddle pan or heavy frying pan with olive oil, and heat until very hot. Cook the eggplant slices for 4 minutes on each side. Cook the zucchini slices for 1 minute on each side.

❖ Place 4 eggplant slices on to a lightly oiled baking tray, and layer the zucchini and tomato slices on top to make little stacks. Finish each stack with an eggplant slice, secure with a cocktail stick, and bake in the oven for 10 minutes.

❖ Meanwhile, make the dressing: Crush the garlic and salt using a pestle and mortar. Add the lemon zest and juice, and whisk with a fork until well mixed. Gradually whisk the oil into the garlic mixture. Season with pepper, and stir in the mint.

❖ Remove the cocktail sticks from the stacks, and spoon the dressing over the top. Scatter fresh basil over the stacks, and serve hot.

each serving contains:
Calories 220 • Protein 3g • Fat 20g (saturated 3g) • Carbohydrates 7g • Fiber 4g • Calories from fat 84% • Excellent source of vitamin C

warm lemon and olive oil beans on rosemary mashed potatoes

serves 4
preparation time: 10 minutes
cooking time: about 20 minutes

these warmed beans with oil and watercress are very simple and extremely effective. I love to infuse oils with herbs and garlic, especially when recipes use tough herbs such as rosemary. It's a great way to add their flavor to a dish without adding the herb.

5 tablespoons extra virgin olive oil
3 sprigs of fresh rosemary
1 garlic clove
2 lbs. potatoes, peeled and cut into chunks
zest of ½ lemon
4 cups (1 lb., 12 ozs.) canned borlotti beans *or* cannellini beans, drained
juice of 1 lemon
handful of fresh parsley, roughly chopped
1 cup (1 oz.) bunch of watercress, roughly chopped
sea salt and freshly ground black pepper

❖ Heat 2 tablespoons of the olive oil in a frying pan. Add the rosemary and garlic, and heat gently for 2 minutes. Remove from the heat, cover, and allow it to infuse while you prepare the mashed potatoes.

❖ Bring a saucepan of water to a boil, add the potato chunks, and simmer for about 15 minutes, until the potatoes are tender. Drain, and return the saucepan to the heat. Dry the potatoes over very low heat, shaking the pan gently.

❖ Remove the rosemary sprigs and garlic from the oil with a slotted spoon, and discard. Add the oil and lemon zest to the potatoes, and mash until they are smooth and creamy. Keep warm.

❖ Put the beans in a saucepan. Drizzle the remaining olive oil and the lemon juice over them, and warm through over a gentle heat. Stir in the parsley and watercress, season well with salt and pepper, and warm through again.

❖ Divide the rosemary mashed potatoes among four warm plates. Put the beans on top, and serve immediately.

each serving contains:
Calories 448 • Protein 17g • Fat 15g (saturated 2g) • Carbohydrates 64g • Fiber 12g • Calories from fat 31% • Good source of vitamin C

warm cumin and coriander spinach on garlic mashed potatoes

serves 4
preparation time: 15 minutes
cooking time: 25 minutes

this dish is comfort food in a bowl. I adore cumin and coriander seeds roasted and ground and mixed through fresh spinach. Their flavor is fabulous and doesn't mask that of the spinach. If you don't have time to mash potatoes, serve the spinach with fresh bread for mopping up the juices.

2 lbs. Idaho or russet potatoes, peeled and cut into chunks
1 garlic clove
5 tablespoons olive oil
sea salt and freshly ground black pepper
2 tablespoons whole-grain mustard (optional)
1 teaspoon cumin seeds
1 teaspoon coriander seeds
2 red onions, finely sliced
7 cups (14 ozs.) fresh spinach leaves
juice of ½ lemon
lemon wedges

❖ Bring a saucepan of water to a boil, add the potato chunks, and simmer for about 15 minutes, until tender. Drain, and return the saucepan to the heat. Dry the potatoes over very low heat, shaking the pan gently.

❖ Using a pestle and mortar, crush the garlic with 2 tablespoons olive oil and a pinch of salt. Add the garlic oil to the potatoes, and mash until they are smooth and creamy. Stir in the mustard, if using, and season well with salt and pepper. Keep warm.

❖ Dry-fry the cumin and coriander seeds over moderate heat in a heavy frying pan, stirring frequently, for a couple of minutes, until they start to pop and turn golden. Coarsely crush the seeds using a pestle and mortar.

❖ Heat the remaining oil in a large saucepan. Add the onions, and cook gently for 10 minutes, until they are soft but not colored. Add the crushed spices and fry, stirring, for 1 minute. Add the spinach leaves, cover, and cook for a couple of minutes, until they wilt. Season with salt and pepper. Add the lemon juice, and toss until the leaves are well coated.

❖ Divide the garlic mashed potatoes among four warm bowls. Top with the spicy spinach, and serve with lemon wedges.

each serving contains:
Calories 345 • Protein 8g • Fat 15g (saturated 2g) • Carbohydrates 46g • Fiber 6g • Calories from fat 40% • Excellent source of vitamin A • Good source of iron, vitamin C and folic acid

balsamic white peach salad
with parsley shortcakes

serves 4
preparation time: 20 minutes
cooking time: 10–12 minutes

I often serve shortcakes instead of bread with salads. The ingredients I use to add flavor to the basic mix depend on the salad. These parsley shortcakes are particularly good filled with the fresh peppery peach salad and its juicy dressing. Replace the parsley with chili pepper or crushed garlic for slightly different shortcakes that go well with a vegan cheese. This recipe is wonderfully versatile. If sweet ingredients such as cinnamon and sugar are substituted for savory ones, the shortcake can be used to create a tasty dessert.

for the shortcakes
1¼ cup (4½ ozs.) plain flour
1½ teaspoons baking powder
pinch of salt
½ teaspoon baking soda
handful of fresh parsley, roughly chopped
2 tablespoons olive oil
1 tablespoon white wine vinegar
6 tablespoons soy milk

½ cup (2½ ozs.) sesame seeds
4 white peaches
4½ cups (9 ozs.) arugula, roughly torn
approx. 1¼ cups (9 ozs.) black olives, pitted
4 tablespoons balsamic vinegar
4 tablespoons olive oil
sea salt and freshly ground black pepper

❖ To make the shortcakes: Preheat the oven to 400°F. Line a baking sheet with baking parchment, or brush it lightly with olive oil. Combine the flour, baking powder, salt, baking soda and parsley in a bowl. In a separate bowl, mix together the oil, vinegar and soy milk. Make a well in the middle of the flour, pour in the liquid, and quickly mix everything together. Do not overmix: The dough is ready when no bits are left in the bowl. Drop 16 tablespoons of the dough onto the prepared baking sheets, spacing them a few inches apart. Flatten them gently, and bake for 10–12 minutes, until golden.

❖ While the shortcakes are baking, dry-fry the sesame seeds in a heavy frying pan over moderate heat. Toss or stirr frequently for a couple of minutes, until golden. Peel and stone the peaches, and cut them into thin slices. Put the slices in a bowl. Add the arugula and olives.

❖ Mix the vinegar and oil together, and season with salt and pepper. Drizzle the dressing over the peaches, add the sesame seeds, and toss to coat the fruit.

❖ While the shortcakes are still warm, split each one in half horizontally. Spoon a little peach salad on one half, and top with the other half. Serve with any leftover salad as an accompaniment.

each serving contains:
Calories 510 • Protein 10g • Fat 35g (saturated 5g) • Carbohydrates 40g • Fiber 7g • Calories from fat 62% • Excellent source of vitamin C • Good source of iron

red cabbage relish with parsley mashed potatoes

serves 4
preparation time: 15 minutes
cooking time: 25 minutes

a little balsamic vinegar and some sweet fruit, such as apples and raisins, can transform the humble cabbage. This dish always makes me think of Christmas—if you are the same you may like to join me in topping it with a large spoonful of cranberry relish. You could even add a handful of dried cranberries to the dish.

3 cups (1½ lbs.) red cabbage
3 tablespoons olive oil
2 tablespoons red wine vinegar
3 tablespoons (1 ozs.) light brown sugar, softened
3 tablespoons red wine
2 York Imperial apples, peeled, cored and thickly sliced
¼ cup (1 oz.) raisins
1 bay leaf
sea salt and freshly ground black pepper
2 lbs. Idaho or russet potatoes, peeled and cut into chunks
2 tablespoons very finely chopped fresh flat-leaf parsley

❖ Remove the outer leaves and core of the cabbage, and slice finely. Heat 1 tablespoon of the olive oil in a saucepan. Stir in the cabbage, then cover and sweat for 5 minutes over very low heat. Add the vinegar, sugar, wine, apples, raisins and bay leaf, and season with salt and pepper. Mix well. Cover the saucepan, and cook gently for 20 minutes, or until the cabbage is soft and sticky but still has a little crunch. Stir frequently to prevent sticking and burning.

❖ Meanwhile, bring a saucepan of water to a boil. Add the potato chunks, and simmer for about 15 minutes, until the potatoes are tender. Drain and return the saucepan to the heat. Dry the potatoes over very low heat, shaking the pan gently. Mash the potatoes, then add the parsley and remaining olive oil. Season with salt and pepper. Divide the parsley mashed potatoes among four warm bowls. Top with the red cabbage relish, and serve.

each serving contains:
Calories 350 • Protein 7g • Fat 9g (saturated 1g) • Carbohydrates 63g • Fiber 8g • Calories from fat 24% • Excellent source of vitamin C • Good source of Vitamin B$_6$ and folic acid

papaya and cilantro salsa on coconut rice

serves 4
preparation time: 20 minutes
cooking time: about 15 minutes

this dish is savory, sweet, tart, hot and cold all at the same time. Coconut rice is the perfect accompaniment to the salsa, but a soft bread will still make it satisfyingly healthy and tasty. One cup of mango slices contains about three-quarters of the adult daily requirement for vitamins A and C. However, I am still more impressed by our friend the papaya, which has a very clever way of helping us digest food. In addition, an average-size papaya provides three times the recommended adult daily requirement for vitamin C, two-thirds of the vitamin A requirement and more than one-third of the potassium requirement.

1¾ cups (14 ozs.) basmati rice
2 tablespoons coconut cream
1 jalapeño chili, seeded and finely chopped
2 large ripe papayas
1 large ripe mango
1 red onion, finely sliced
grated zest and juice of 2 limes
2 handfuls of cilantro, roughly chopped

❖ Bring a large saucepan of water to a boil, and add the rice and coconut cream. Simmer for 15 minutes, or until the rice is tender.

❖ Meanwhile, put the jalapeño chili into a bowl. Peel the papaya, remove the seeds, and cut the flesh into bite-size chunks. Add the papaya to the jalapeño. Peel the mango, and use a sharp knife to slice the flesh away from the pit. Cut the flesh into bite-size chunks. Add the mango, onion, lime zest and juice and half the cilantro to the papaya, and mix together well.

❖ Divide the coconut rice among four warm bowls, and spoon the salsa on top. Scatter the remaining cilantro over each bowl, and serve.

each serving contains:
Calories 450 • Protein 9g • Fat 2g (saturated 1.5g) • Carbohydrates 97g • Fiber 4g •Calories from fat 5% • Excellent source of vitamin C • Good source of vitamin A

chili and cilantro corn fritters with tomato sauce

serves 4
preparation time: 20 minutes
cooking time: 15 minutes

although I am not a great fan of deep-frying, I recognize that many people enjoy a fritter from time to time, so I have included a couple of such recipes to satisfy those cravings. To make these fritters a little different, I have included a few chopped and ground almonds to add flavor, crunch and extra protein. The addition of lots of red chili peppers and cilantro ensures that each fritter is packed with color and flavor. Eat the fritters as soon as they are cooked—they do not improve with age.

for the tomato sauce
1 tablespoon olive oil
1 shallot, finely sliced
1¾ cups (14 ozs.) canned tomatoes
1 tablespoon cilantro, roughly chopped
sea salt and freshly ground black pepper

½ cup (2 ozs.) almonds
1½ cups (8 ozs.) plain flour
½ cup (2 ozs.) ground almonds
2 teaspoons salt
1 cup (8 fl. ozs.) water
1½ cups (12 ozs.) canned corn kernels
3 red chili peppers, seeded and finely chopped
2 teaspoons chili powder
pinch of freshly ground black pepper
2 tablespoons cilantro, roughly chopped
vegetable oil, for deep-frying

❖ Preheat the oven to 300°F. Line a plate or baking tray with paper towels. To make the tomato sauce: Heat the olive oil in a frying pan. Add the shallot, and sweat over a gentle heat for 2–3 minutes, until softened. Add the tomatoes, and simmer for 5 minutes. Stir in the cilantro, and season to taste with salt and pepper. Keep warm.

❖ Dry-fry the almonds in a heavy frying pan over moderate heat. Toss or stir frequently for 5 minutes, until golden. Let the nuts cool a little, then chop them.

❖ Put the flour, ground almonds and salt in a food processor. Add the water, and process to a thick batter. Transfer to a bowl. Add the corn kernels, chopped almonds, chili peppers, chili powder, pepper and cilantro; mix well.

❖ Heat the vegetable oil to about 375°F in a deep fryer or a deep, heavy saucepan. To test the temperature, drop a little batter into the oil—it should sizzle immediately. Carefully drop a few tablespoons of the mixture into the hot oil, and fry for a few minutes, until golden brown. Drain on paper towels, and keep warm in the oven. Repeat the process with the remaining mixture. Serve immediately with the tomato sauce as an accompaniment.

each serving contains:
Calories 633 • Protein 15g • Fat 34g (saturated 4g) •
Carbohydrates 72g • Fiber 6g • Calories from fat 48% • Excellent
source of vitamin E • Good source of vitamin C

grilled eggplant with black olive dressing

serves 4
preparation time: 15 minutes
cooking time: 10 minutes

eggplant has such a satisfying texture—the bigger the slices, the better the dish. And thick ones grill very well. The secret is not to panic when the vegetable initially cries out for oil. Allow it to carry on cooking, however dry it may appear, and it will gradually release its own juices. Because of its bland flavor, eggplant needs a few pungent additions, hence the sauce of black olives, capers and garlic.

2 garlic cloves
12 black olives, pitted and roughly chopped
4 teaspoons small capers
handful of fresh flat-leaf parsley, roughly chopped
handful of cilantro, roughly chopped
2 tablespoons extra virgin olive oil, plus extra for grilling and drizzling
2 large eggplants, each cut into 4 slices
½ cup (2 ozs.) mixed baby salad leaves, roughly torn
sea salt and freshly ground black pepper
handful of cilantro, to serve

❖ Preheat the oven to 400°F. Crush the garlic using a pestle and mortar. Add the chopped olives and capers, and crush to a thick, lumpy paste. Add the parsley and cilantro, then whisk in the 2 tablespoons of olive oil with a fork.

❖ Brush a griddle pan or heavy frying pan with a little olive oil, and heat until very hot. Brush the eggplant slices with a little oil. Grill the slices for about 5 minutes on each side, until charred and cooked. Remove from the pan.

❖ Mix together the salad leaves, drizzle a little extra virgin olive oil over them, and season with salt and pepper. Divide the leaves among four plates, top with the eggplant slices, and drizzle the dressing over the top. Serve topped with a few cilantro leaves.

each serving contains:
Calories 105 • Protein 1.5g • Fat 10g (saturated 1.5g) •
Carbohydrates 3g • Fiber 3g • Calories from fat 84%

spanish potato gratin

serves 4
preparation time: 15 minutes
cooking time: 35 minutes

my brother's Spanish girlfriend often comes to stay with us in England. She and I play in the kitchen with ingredients that she is familiar with to create a meal that we both love. This recipe was developed one evening before we rushed off to the cinema. It is one of those dishes that you can further develop each time you cook it. The brown bread crumbs can come from any type of brown bread, as long as it is vegan. And you could add peppers—or other vegetables such as zucchini and eggplant—to the tomato base. It all depends on the available ingredients and how long you wish to spend in the kitchen. Serve with a fresh green salad.

2¼ cups (10½ ozs.) potatoes, peeled and cut into chunks
3 tablespoons olive oil
1 large onion, sliced
1 garlic clove, finely chopped
1⅓ cups (14 ozs.) canned plum tomatoes, roughly chopped
4 tablespoons (2 ozs.) green olives, pitted
4 tablespoons (2 ozs.) black olives, pitted
2 tablespoons (1 oz.) fresh flat-leaf parsley, finely chopped
1 tablespoon (1 oz.) fresh thyme leaves, finely chopped
sea salt and freshly ground black pepper
¼ cup (2½ ozs.) brown bread crumbs

❖ Preheat the oven to 375°F. Bring a saucepan of water to a boil. Add the potato chunks, and simmer for about 15 minutes, until tender. Drain, and return the saucepan to the heat. Dry the potatoes over very low heat, shaking the pan gently. Mash the potatoes.

❖ Heat half the oil in a large saucepan. Add the onion and garlic, and sauté over moderate heat for 5 minutes, or until the onion is soft and golden. Mix in the tomatoes, olives, half the parsley and thyme, and season with salt and pepper. Spoon the mixture into an ovenproof dish. Top with the mashed potatoes, and scatter the bread crumbs and remaining parsley and thyme over them. Drizzle the remaining oil over the top, and bake in the oven for 15 minutes, or until the potatoes are golden. Serve immediately.

each serving contains:
Calories 240 • Protein 5g • Fat 12g (saturated 2g) • Carbohydrates 28g • Fiber 5g • Calories from fat 47% • Excellent source of vitamin C

roasted potatoes and parsnips with chestnuts and sage

serves 4
preparation time: 20 minutes
cooking time: 35–40 minutes

there are so many ingredients that make life easier for the modern cook. Cooked and peeled chestnuts, conveniently vacuum-packed to keep them fresh until you want to use them, are an example; then are well worth keeping in the cupboard. Serve these root vegetables in warm bowls with fresh green vegetables, and topped with a large spoonful of lingonberry relish in the center. Substitute a relish made from cranberries if you wish—lingonberries are their Swedish sisters. If you are using old parsnips, remove the woody cores.

2 tablespoons olive oil
1 lb. potatoes, peeled and cut into chunks
1 lb. parsnips, peeled and cut into chunks
1 cup (7 ozs.) cooked peeled chestnuts
2 large handfuls of fresh sage, roughly chopped
4 tablespoons relish

❖ Preheat the oven to 425°F. Heat the olive oil on top of the stove in a heavy roasting pan. Add the potatoes and parsnips, and sauté over high heat for 5 minutes, until they start to brown. Transfer the dish to the oven, and roast for 20 minutes. Add the chestnuts and fresh sage, and roast for another 20–25 minutes.
❖ Divide the vegetables among four warm bowls. Top each serving with a spoonful of lingonberry relish, and serve.

each serving contains:
Calories 290 • Protein 5g • Fat 8g (saturated 1g) • Carbohydrates 52g • Fiber 8g • Calories from fat 26% • Good source of vitamin B$_1$ (thiamin), vitamin C and folic acid

salad of ciabatta croutons with avocado, grapefruit and vinaigrette

serves 4
preparation time: 15 minutes
cooking time: 10 minutes

the croutons make an excellent crunchy contrast to the soft avocado. Avocados are ripe if they yield when you press the skin gently. Keep them in a fruit bowl if you wish to speed up the ripening process. Once ripe, they can be stored in the fridge.

4 slices ciabatta bread, about 1" thick
2 tablespoons extra virgin olive oil
2 ripe grapefruit
4 ripe avocados

for the vinaigrette
5 tablespoons extra virgin olive oil
2 tablespoons white wine vinegar
1 teaspoon coarse-grain mustard
sea salt and freshly ground black pepper

❖ Preheat the oven to 400°F. Cut the slices of bread into 1" squares, and place them on a baking tray in a single layer. Drizzle the oil over them. Bake in the oven for 10 minutes, until golden, turning the croutons once.

❖ Peel the grapefruit, working around the fruit with a sharp knife. Make sure you remove the pith. Then cut the segments of flesh away from the membrane with the knife. Put the segments in a bowl. Slice the avocados in half lengthwise, and remove the stones. Peel the avocados, then slice the flesh, and add it to the grapefruit.

❖ To make the vinaigrette: Put all the ingredients in a screw-top jar, and shake vigorously until thoroughly blended. The dressing must be slightly thick.

❖ Drizzle the vinaigrette over the fruit, toss, and season well with salt and pepper. Add the croutons to the salad, and serve.

each serving contains:
Calories 535 • Protein 5g • Fat 48g (saturated 10g) • Carbohydrates 20g • Fiber 6.5g • Calories from fat 81% • Excellent source of vitamins C and E

spicy satay on white bread

serves 4
preparation time: 5 minutes
cooking time: 10 minutes

I love snacks like this one. If you want to make the sandwiches a little more colorful, grate lots of fresh carrot over the satay filling. This peanut spread also makes a fabulous dip—just add a little more water to make it slightly looser in texture. You should be able to find creamed coconut in Asian grocery stores.

4 tablespoons peanut butter
3 garlic cloves, crushed
1 green chili pepper, seeded and chopped
½ cup (5 fl. ozs.) water
¼ cup (1¾ ozs.) creamed coconut
1 tablespoon soy sauce
freshly ground black pepper
8 thick slices white bread
2 spring onions, finely sliced

❖ Put the peanut butter, garlic and chili pepper into a saucepan with the water. Heat gently, stirring, until smooth. Add the creamed coconut and soy sauce, season with the pepper, and mix thoroughly.

❖ Spread a thick layer of the satay on 4 slices of bread. Scatter the spring onions over the satay, and cover with the remaining slices of bread.

each serving contains:
Calories 375 • Protein 12g • Fat 18g (saturated 9g) •Carbohydrates 42g • Fiber 2.5g • Calories from fat 45%

basmati and wild rice salad

serves 4
preparation time: 15 minutes
cooking time: 10–15 minutes

the combination of beets and horseradish gives this salad a delicious flavor kick. Make the salad in advance and keep it in the fridge. The flavor improves with time, so you could prepare it in the evening for lunch the following day.

10 tablespoons (5 ozs.) basmati rice
4 tablespoons (2 ozs.) wild rice
7 radishes, thinly sliced
1 red pepper, seeded and cut into thin strips
2 medium-size cooked beets, cut into small chunks
1 red onion, diced
large handful of fresh chives, finely chopped

for the dressing
4 tablespoons white wine vinegar
2 tablespoons creamed horseradish
whole-grain mustard
1 teaspoon turbinado sugar
1 teaspoon sea salt
1 teaspoon freshly ground black pepper
4 tablespoons extra virgin olive oil

❖ Cook the rice according to the instructions on the packet. Let cool, then transfer to a serving bowl.
❖ Meanwhile, make the dressing: Put all the ingredients in a screw-top jar, and shake vigorously until throughly blended.
❖ Add the radishes, red pepper, beets and onion to the rice, and mix well. Scatter the fresh chives over the top. Pour the dressing over the rice, mix well, and serve.

each serving contains:
Calories 320 • Protein 5g • Fat 12g (saturated 1.5g) • Carbohydrates 47g • Fiber 2g • Calories from fat 34% • Excellent source of vitamin C • Good source of vitamins B_1 (thiamin), B_3 (niacin), B_6 and E

winter green salad with very garlicky vinaigrette

serves 4
preparation time: 10 minutes

most of us tend to be lazy when it comes to making fresh green salads. So many bags of mixed leaves are available in supermarkets that we don't spend any time making our own salads. Choose leaves with different flavors, colors and textures and you will be delighted with the finished result. If your supermarket doesn't stock the ones in this recipe, ask your local greengrocer for a selection.

This salad is also good with big, crunchy croutons tossed through it (see page 97).

for the very garlicky vinaigrette
3 garlic cloves, crushed
2 tablespoons Dijon mustard
6 tablespoons extra virgin olive oil

2$\frac{1}{4}$ cups (4$\frac{1}{2}$ ozs.) arugula
2$\frac{1}{4}$ cups (4$\frac{1}{2}$ ozs.) watercress
1 cup (2 ozs.) red leaf lettuce
1 cup (2 ozs.) romaine leaves
2$\frac{3}{4}$ cups (5 ozs.) radicchio
2$\frac{3}{4}$ cups (5 ozs.) endive

❖ First, make the garlicky vinaigrette: Put all the ingredients in a screw-top jar, and shake vigorously until thoroughly blended. Set aside.
❖ Roughly tear the arugula, watercress, red leaf lettuce and romaine leaves, and put them in a salad bowl. Finely slice the radicchio and endive, add them to the bowl, and mix well.
❖ Pour the dressing over the salad, toss, and serve.

each serving contains:
Calories 173 • Protein 2g • Fat 17g (saturated 2.5g) • Carbohydrates 2g • Fiber 2g • Calories from fat 91% • Good source of vitamin C

a very modern waldorf salad

serves 4
preparation time: 15 minutes

I have always loved the combination of fruit and nuts and many of my recipes contain both ingredients in many different guises. This salad is easy to make, but very effective. It is often difficult to get the balance of ingredients in a simple recipe right so that the flavors complement, rather than compete with, one another. The crunchy pears and nuts contrast with the soft raisins, and the carrot adds color as well as being a good source of vitamins. Serve the salad with a fruit bread.

juice of 1 lemon
1/2 cup (4 fl. ozs.) water
4 ripe pears, cored and sliced
4 sticks celery, thinly sliced
3 carrots, grated
1 1/4 cups (4 1/2 ozs.) walnuts, coarsely chopped
1 1/4 cups (5 1/2 ozs.) raisins
1 tablespoon fresh mint leaves, roughly chopped

for the dressing
2 tablespoons red wine vinegar
1 teaspoon Dijon mustard
4 tablespoons walnut oil
1 tablespoon vegetable oil
sea salt and freshly ground black pepper

❖ Combine the lemon juice and water in a large bowl. Add the pears, and toss until they are coated. Let sit for 10 minutes, then drain.
❖ To make the dressing: Put all the ingredients in a screw-top jar, and shake vigorously until thoroughly blended. Set aside.
❖ Put the celery, carrots, walnuts and raisins in a serving bowl. Add the pears and fresh mint. Pour the dressing over the salad, and serve.

each serving contains:
Calories 520 • Protein 6g • Fat 36g (saturated 3g) • Carbohydrates 46g • Fiber 7g • Calories from fat 62% • Excellent source of vitamin A • Good source of vitamin C

sandwiches

pita bread with garlic cream and fresh lime

serves 4
preparation time: 15 minutes

if you are looking for sandwich fillings that are more interesting than nut butter or salad, the suggestions on the next few pages are for you. And, of course, many of the dishes in this chapter and the previous one can be adapted to fill sandwiches.

3 slices white bread, crusts removed
1 tablespoon tahini
2 garlic cloves, crushed
juice of 1 lime
⅔ cup extra virgin olive oil
sea salt and freshly ground black pepper
2 teaspoons sesame seeds
4 pitas, split in half
1 head of romaine lettuce, finely shredded
handful of fresh mint leaves, roughly chopped
1 lime, cut into chunks

❖ Tear the white bread into chunks. Put the bread, tahini, garlic and lime juice in a food processor, and process to a coarse paste. With the motor running, gradually add the olive oil. Transfer the garlic spread to a bowl, season well with salt and pepper, and mix in the sesame seeds.

❖ Cut each pita in half horizontally, then cut each half open to make 8 pockets. Pack a little lettuce inside each half, spoon a little garlic spread onto the lettuce, and scatter some fresh mint over the spread. Serve with wedges of lime.

each serving contains:
Calories 540 • Protein 10g • Fat 32g (saturated 5g) •
Carbohydrates 55g • Fiber 3g • Calories from fat 54%

thai vegetables
in fresh herb bread

serves 4
preparation time: 20 minutes

it's always a refreshing change to make a dressing that has very little oil. If anything really annoys me in restaurants, it's when salads arrive at the table swimming in a tasteless oily dressing. To avoid any embarrassment to the restaurant staff or my friends, I always order dressing on the side so that I can add as much or as little as I like. If you want this one to have more of a kick, add a few seeds from the chili pepper. The prepared vegetables will keep, covered, in the fridge for at least two hours. I have recommended an herb bread in this recipe, but pumpkin bread or any other specialty bread will do just as well.

2 carrots, grated
4 spring onions, trimmed and finely sliced
1½ cups (4½ ozs.) sugar snap peas, cut into thin strips
½ cup (4½ ozs.) yellow cherry tomatoes, halved
3 tablespoons fresh basil leaves, preferably Thai basil
8 slices fresh herb bread

for the dressing
2 red chili peppers, seeded and finely sliced
½ cup (4 fl. ozs.) coconut milk
juice of 1 lime
2 teaspoons sesame oil
sea salt and freshly ground black pepper

❖ Mix the carrots, onions, peas and tomatoes in a bowl. Stack 6 basil leaves together, roll them into a cigar shape, and cut into thin strips. Add the basil strips to the vegetables. Repeat with the remaining basil.

❖ Put all the dressing ingredients in a screw-top jar, and shake vigorously until well blended. Drizzle the dressing over the vegetables, toss well, and season to taste with salt and pepper.

❖ Spread the Thai vegetables on 4 slices of bread, and cover with the remaining slices.

each serving contains:
Calories 300 • Protein 10g • Fat 6g (saturated 3g) • Carbohydrates 54g • Fiber 3.5g • Calories from fat 18% • Good source of vitamins A and C

avocado butter with tomato relish in focaccia

serves 4
preparation time: 20 minutes

it is almost worth making a double quantity of this fabulous tomato relish and storing some in the fridge to go in other sandwiches or to serve with vegetable dishes. It will keep for at least two days (much longer without the herbs). To transform the avocado butter into a dip, add a skinned and chopped ripe tomato, a few tablespoons of soy yogurt and a little more lime juice to the mixture. You may also need to add a little more Tabasco sauce, as the dip should have a bit of a kick to it.

for the tomato relish
15 sun-dried tomatoes, finely diced
2 garlic cloves, crushed
large handful of fresh basil leaves
large handful of fresh thyme leaves, finely chopped
about 2 tablespoons extra virgin olive oil

for the avocado butter
2 ripe avocados
juice of ½ lime
1–2 dashes of Tabasco sauce
sea salt and freshly ground black pepper
4 small focaccia _or_ 2 large focaccia, halved

❖ First, make the tomato relish: Put the tomatoes and garlic in a bowl. Stack 6 basil leaves together, roll them into a cigar shape, and slice into thin strips. Repeat with the remaining basil leaves. Mix the basil and thyme into the tomatoes. Stir in enough oil to make a relish texture.

❖ To make the avocado butter: Slice each avocado in half lengthwise, and remove the pit. Peel the avocadoes, then chop the flesh, and put it in a food processor. Add the lime juice and Tabasco sauce to taste. Season with salt and pepper. Process until smooth.

❖ Cut each focaccia or half focaccia in half horizontally. Spread a layer of avocado butter on 4 halves, top with the tomato relish, and cover with the remaining halves.

each serving contains:
Calories 445 • Protein 2g • Fat 36g (saturated 5.5g) • Carbohydrates 24g • Fiber 2.5g • Calories from fat 72% • Excellent source of vitamin E

carrots with mint and lime dressing in pita bread

serves 4
preparation time: 10 minutes

the combination of mint, lime (or lemon) and olive oil makes a wonderfully refreshing dressing for the carrots. This dish would also be delicious with a little pureed chickpeas (see page 35) spread in the pita pockets and a big handful of fresh watercress squeezed in.

1½ lbs. carrots, coarsely grated
1 tablespoon olive oil
1 tablespoon fresh lime or lemon juice
large handful of fresh mint leaves, roughly chopped
sea salt and freshly ground black pepper
4 pitas

❖ Put the carrots in a bowl. Combine the olive oil, lime or lemon juice and mint leaves in a small bowl, and season with salt and pepper. Pour the dressing over the carrots, and mix well.
❖ Cut each pita in half horizontally, then cut each half open to make 8 pockets. Pack the pita pockets with the carrot salad.

each serving contains:
Calories 300 • Protein 8g • Fat 4g (saturated 0.7g) • Carbohydrates 62g • Fiber 6g • Calories from fat 12% • Excellent source of vitamin A • Good source of vitamin C

main courses

roasted garlic polenta
with sautéed tomatoes

serves 4
preparation time: 20 minutes
cooking time: 55 minutes

roasted garlic has a sweet and mellow flavor that is perfect in creamy polenta. Topped with basil and mixed tomatoes dressed with olive oil, it's a dish you will enjoy again and again.

2 garlic bulbs
2 bay leaves
sprig of fresh thyme
3 tablespoons extra virgin olive oil
sea salt and freshly ground black pepper
¾ cup (4½ ozs.) polenta
2 cups (2½ ozs.) fresh basil leaves
4½ cups (2¼ lbs.) mixed yellow, cherry and plum
   tomatoes
2 cups (1 pint) water

❖ Preheat the oven to 350°F. Bring a saucepan of water to a boil. Slice the garlic bulbs n half horizontally. Add them to the boiling water, and simmer for about 8 minutes, until they are tender.

❖ Use a draining spoon to drain the garlic and transfer it to an ovenproof dish. Add the bay leaves and thyme, then drizzle 1 tablespoon olive oil over the garlic. Season with salt and pepper, and bake for 45 minutes.

❖ Meanwhile, discard the water from the saucepan, and rinse out the pan. Pour 1 pint water into the pan, and add 1 teaspoon salt. Heat until simmering, then add the polenta by letting it run through your fingers in a thin stream while stirring continuously to prevent lumps from forming.

❖ When all the polenta is added, cover the pan, and simmer for 30 minutes, stirring every 5 minutes. The polenta is cooked when it comes away from the sides of the saucepan in a smooth, thick paste.

❖ Squeeze the flesh out of the garlic, and add half of it to the polenta. Season well, and stir in half the basil.

❖ Quarter the large tomatoes, and cut the cherry tomatoes in half. Heat the remaining olive oil and garlic flesh in a frying pan over a gentle heat for 1 minute. Add the tomatoes, and cook gently for 10 minutes. Add the remaining basil to the tomatoes along with salt and pepper to taste. Serve the polenta topped with the hot tomatoes.

each serving contains:
Calories 240 • Protein 5g • Fat 10g (saturated 1.5g) •
Carbohydrates 31g • Fiber 3g • Calories from fat 38% • Excellent
source of vitamins A and C • Good source of vitamin E

tomato and pine nut linguine with caramelized lemon

serves 4
preparation time: 15 minutes, plus marinating time
cooking time: 10–12 minutes

the flavors in this dish are fresh and simple, with hot golden lemon slices to squeeze over the pasta just before you eat it. Serve with French bread.

1 lb. ripe, juicy vine-ripened tomatoes, quartered
½ cup (1¾ ozs.) pine nuts
2 large handfuls of fresh basil leaves
1 tablespoon balsamic vinegar
3 tablespoons light fruity olive oil
sea salt and freshly ground black pepper
14 ozs. linguine (or other pasta of your choice)
½ lemon, thickly sliced from the top

❖ Put the tomatoes in a large bowl. Add the pine nuts and half the fresh basil. Drizzle the balsamic vinegar and 2 tablespoons of the olive oil over the top. Season with salt and lots of pepper, and mix well. Let sit at least 30 minutes.

❖ Bring a large saucepan of water to a boil, and cook the linguine according to the instructions on the packet. Drain.

❖ While the linguine is cooking, heat the remaining olive oil in a frying pan. Fry the lemon slices for 1 minute on each side, or until they start to turn golden.

❖ Add the linguine to the marinated tomatoes, and toss well. Scatter the remaining fresh basil over the top, and serve with the hot lemon slices.

each serving contains:
Calories 535 • Protein 15g • Fat 19g (saturated 2g) •
Carbohydrates 81g • Fiber 4.5g • Calories from fat 32% • Excellent
source of vitamin C • Good source of vitamins A and E

gnocchi with tomatoes and fresh mint

serves 4
preparation time: 10 minutes
cooking time: 15 minutes

it's best to use fresh tomatoes in this recipe, but canned tomatoes will work if they are unavailable. Remember to check the label on the packet of gnocchi to make sure that they do not contain dairy products.

4 tablespoons extra virgin olive oil
1 garlic clove, finely chopped
1 shallot, finely chopped
1 teaspoon turbinado sugar
4 tablespoons vegetable stock
3 cups (24½ ozs.) canned crushed tomatoes
sea salt and pepper
14 ozs. potato gnocchi
handful of fresh mint leaves, roughly chopped *or* fresh
   basil leaves, torn

❖ Heat half the olive oil in a frying pan. Add the garlic, shallot, sugar and stock. Cover, and cook gently for about 10 minutes, or until the onion has softened and the liquid has evaporated. Add the tomatoes, cover, and cook for another 5 minutes. Season to taste with salt and pepper, and add the remaining olive oil. Mix well.

❖ Bring a large saucepan of water to a boil, and cook the gnocchi for approximately 4 minutes. They will rise to the surface when they are cooked. Remove the gnocchi with a slotted spoon, and drain them on paper towels while you empty the saucepan. Return the gnocchi to the saucepan, add the sauce, and mix well. Scatter fresh mint or basil over the top, and serve.

each serving contains:
Calories 295 • Protein 6g • Fat 12g (saturated 1.5g) •
Carbohydrates 42g • Fiber 1g • Calories from fat 36% • Excellent
source of vitamin C

mixed mushrooms
and tofu pasta

serves 4
preparation time: 20 minutes
cooking time: 20 minutes

the tofu in this recipe adds a little creaminess to coat the pasta. There are many health benefits to eating this soybean product, not the least of which is its high percentage of protein. It is eaten in vast quantities in Japan, along with other products of the bean such as shoyu and miso. Try to include a few oriental mushrooms if they are available.

1 lb., 2 ozs. mixed mushrooms, such as button and
    shiitake
4 garlic cloves, coarsely chopped
1 large onion, sliced
3 tablespoons olive oil
1¼ cup (4½ ozs.) pine nuts
2 tablespoons roughly torn fresh basil leaves
2 tablespoons finely chopped fresh thyme leaves
2 tablespoons finely chopped fresh flat-leaf parsley
1 lb. firm tofu
juice of ½ lemon
14 ozs. pasta of your choice
sea salt and freshly ground black pepper
handful of mixed fresh basil leaves, fresh thyme leaves
    and fresh flat-leaf parsley, finely chopped

❖ Slice any large mushrooms into chunks. Put the mushrooms, garlic and onion in a food processor. Process to a chunky paste.
❖ Heat the olive oil in a frying pan. Add the mushroom paste, and sauté over moderate heat for 5 minutes. Stir in the pine nuts, basil, thyme and parsley, and cook for another 5 minutes.
❖ Put the tofu in the food processor, and process just enough to make a coarse puree —it must not be too creamy. Add the tofu and lemon juice to the mushrooms. Stir well and cook, covered, over moderate heat for 10 minutes.

❖ Bring a large saucepan of water to a boil, and cook the pasta according to the instructions on the packet. Drain, return the pasta to the saucepan, and add the mushrooms. Toss well, and season with salt and pepper. Divide among four warm bowls. Scatter fresh basil, thyme and parsley over the top, and serve.

each serving contains:
Calories 670 • Protein 28g • Fat 28g (saturated 2g) • Carbohydrates 80g • Fiber 5g • Calories from fat 38% • Excellent source of vitamin E • Good source of vitamins B_1 (thiamin) and B_3 (niacin)

spaghetti with tomato sauce

serves 4
preparation time: 20 minutes
cooking time: 50 minutes

every vegan cook book needs a good tomato sauce—and if you are going to do it properly, it should be made with fresh tomatoes (always remove the skins when cooking fresh tomatoes). I have also added some sun-dried to make the tomato flavor slightly more intense. You could make double the quantity and keep half in the fridge for a few days. It's perfect for serving with vegetables or in lasagnas, as well as with spaghetti and other pastas.

2¼ lbs. vine-ripened tomatoes
2 tablespoons olive oil
3 garlic cloves, crushed
2 large onions
2 tablespoons fresh basil leaves, roughly chopped
2 tablespoons fresh thyme leaves, chopped
3 sprigs of fresh rosemary
1 teaspoon chili powder
pinch of turbinado sugar
sea salt and freshly ground black pepper
½ cup (2 ozs.) sun-dried tomatoes, coarsely chopped
14 ozs. spaghetti

❖ Put the tomatoes in a bowl, and cover with boiling water. After 20 seconds in the boiling water plunge them straight into cold water. Drain and skin the tomatoes, then roughly chop their flesh.

❖ Heat the oil in a large saucepan. Add the garlic and onions, and sauté over moderate heat for 5 minutes, until soft and golden. Add the tomatoes, basil, thyme, rosemary and chili powder, and simmer gently, uncovered, for about 45 minutes, until reduced to a thick sauce, stirring occasionally. Mix in the sugar, and season to taste with salt and pepper. Add the sun-dried tomatoes, and heat through for a few minutes. Remove the rosemary sprigs.

❖ Bring a large saucepan of water to a boil, and cook the spaghetti according to the instructions on the packet. Drain. Divide the spaghetti among four warm bowls, spoon the tomato sauce over the top, and serve.

each serving contains:
Calories 525 • Protein 15g • Fat 15g
(saturated 2g) • Carbohydrates 88g •
Fiber 6g • Calories from fat 26% • Good
source of vitamins A, C and E

roasted garlic
and walnut linguine

serves 4
preparation time: 20 minutes
cooking time: 1 ³/₄ hours

my father lived in Rome for three years, and I frequently flew to Italy to see him. This dish is based on one of the most memorable vegan meals we ate together. There may seem to be a lot of garlic, but don't panic—the flavor is sweet and subtle after 1 ½ hours of roasting.

2 heads of garlic
4 tablespoons vegetable stock (see page 62)
2 tablespoons olive oil
½ cup (2½ ozs.) walnuts, roughly chopped
1 tablespoon ground walnuts
2 tablespoons fresh flat-leaf parsley, roughly chopped
sea salt and freshly ground black pepper
14 ozs. linguine

❖ Preheat the oven to 350°F. Cut the heads of garlic in half horizontally, and put them in a roasting tin. Drizzle the stock over the garlic, and roast for 1¼–1½ hours, until soft and tender. Squeeze all the garlic flesh out of the cloves. Mash half the flesh with 1 tablespoon olive oil to make a puree. Reserve the remaining flesh.

❖ Put the walnuts on a baking tray in a single layer, and roast for 5 minutes, turning once.

❖ Heat the remaining oil in a large saucepan. Add the garlic puree and ground walnuts, and sauté over moderate heat for 5 minutes. Add the roasted walnuts, the remaining garlic and the parsley. Season with salt and pepper.

❖ Bring a large saucepan of water to a boil, and cook the linguine according to the instructions on the packet. Drain. Toss the linguine with the garlic and walnut sauce, and heat gently to warm through. Divide among four warm bowls, and serve immediately.

each serving contains:
Calories 440 • Protein 13.5g • Fat 11g (saturated 1.5g) •
Carbohydrates 76g • Fiber 3.5g • Calories from fat 23%

thai noodles with chili and lemon grass dressing

serves 4
preparation time: 15 minutes
cooking time: 10 minutes

i would prefer the vegetables in this recipe to remain raw, in order to gain the maximum nutritional benefit, but I've blanched them as a compromise. Lemon grass will really make the dish sing, but if you do not have any, use lemon zest with a little grated fresh ginger. You can use any type of dried noodles that you'd like, as long as they don't contain egg.

9-oz. packet dried medium noodles
1¼ cups (7 ozs.) asparagus, trimmed
1½ cups (4½ ozs.) snow peas
2 carrots, finely sliced
1 red chili pepper, seeded and finely sliced
3 spring onions, finely sliced
½ cup (1¾ ozs.) cashews, chopped

for the dressing
1 stick lemon grass, finely chopped
handful of cilantro, roughly chopped
1 red chili pepper, seeded and finely chopped
1 tablespoon sesame oil
2 tablespoons extra virgin olive oil
1 tablespoon soy sauce
juice of 1 lime
sea salt and freshly ground black pepper

to serve
1 red chili pepper, seeded and finely sliced
5 spring onions, sliced lengthwise into thin strips

❖ Bring a large saucepan of water to a boil, and cook the noodles for 10 minutes. Drain, then rinse them in cold running water. Set aside.
❖ While the noodles are cooking, bring another pan of water to a boil. Add the asparagus, and blanch for a couple of minutes. Remove the spears with a slotted

spoon, plunge them into a bowl of cold water, then drain and slice diagonally. Blanch the snow peas in the same way for 1 minute. Drain.

❖ To make the dressing: Put all the ingredients in a screw-top jar, and shake vigorously until well blended.

❖ Put the vegetables, cashews and noodles in a serving bowl. Add the dressing, and toss together well. Scatter pepper slices the chili and spring onion strips over the top, and serve.

each serving contains:
Calories 405 • Protein 8g • Fat 15g (saturated 2.5g) • Carbohydrates 57g • Fiber 3g • Calories from fat 33% • Good source of vitamins A and C

vegan sushi with avocado and cucumber

serves 4
preparation time: 20 minutes
cooking time: 10 minutes, plus standing time

the great thing about sushi is that it does not have to involve eating lots of fish. You can enjoy it made with avocado and cucumber, or other fruits and vegetables. The combination of sweet and sour—sugar and vinegar—works well with rice and fruit or vegetables. These vegan sushi can look really stunning. For a dramatic effect, serve them on a large dark blue or black plate with the accompaniments in little dishes at the center of the plate. You can find dashi-kombu in Japanese markets and health food stores.

½ cucumber, peeled
2 tablespoons turbinado sugar
4 tablespoons rice wine vinegar
piece of dashi-konbu
1 cup (8 ozs.) Japanese sushi rice
2 cups (16 fl. ozs.) water
1–2 teaspoons wasabi paste
3 tablespoons pickled ginger
1 large avocado
juice of ½ lime
bowls of pickled ginger, soy sauce and wasabi paste

❖ Halve the cucumber lengthwise, and scoop out the seeds with a teaspoon. Slice into thin strips with a vegetable peeler, and put in a bowl. Mix the sugar and vinegar in a small bowl, and drizzle half the dressing over the cucumber slices. Reserve the remaining dressing.

❖ Put the dashi-konbu, rice and water into a large saucepan. Bring to a boil, then remove the dashi-konbu. Cover, and simmer the rice for 10 minutes, until cooked—it should still have a little bite left in it. Remove from the heat, and add the remaining dressing. Let stand, still covered, for 15 minutes. Transfer the rice to a bowl, and let cool. Mold the rice into walnut-size balls, and top each ball with a little wasabi and pickled ginger.

❖ Slice the avocado in half lengthwise, and remove the pit. Peel, and slice the flesh into short, thin strips. Drizzle lime juice over the strips. Top each rice ball with an avocado strip or 2 cucumber slices. Arrange the sushi on a large plate, and serve with bowls of pickled ginger, soy sauce and wasabi paste.

each serving contains:
Calories 315 • Protein 5g • Fat 8g (saturated 1.5g) • Carbohydrates 58g • Fiber 2g • Calories from fat 24%

red cabbage with sake on rice noodles

serves 4
preparation time: 20 minutes
cooking time: 25 minutes

rice noodles are one of those ingredients that you either love or hate. Prepared correctly, they can be delicious. They take very little time to cook, but it is always advisable to follow the instructions on the packet rather than a recipe, because the instructions vary depending on the size of the noodle. Cook the vegetables for as long as you like. Some people enjoy them with a little bite, others prefer them to be soft.

2 tablespoons sesame oil
2 garlic cloves, crushed
1 red cabbage, finely sliced
8 spring onions, finely sliced
5 carrots, finely sliced
5 celery sticks
4 tablespoons soy sauce
4 tablespoons sake
1½ cups (12¼ ozs.) rice noodles
1 bunch of chives, finely chopped

❖ Heat the sesame oil in a saucepan. Add the garlic, cabbage, spring onions, carrots and celery, and sauté over moderate heat for 10 minutes, until the vegetables are soft. Stir in the soy sauce and sake. Simmer, covered, for an additional 15 minutes, or until the vegetables are cooked to your taste.

❖ Meanwhile, cook the rice noodles according to the instructions on the packet.

❖ Transfer the noodles to a large warm bowl, and spoon the vegetables on top. Scatter fresh chives over top, and serve.

each serving contains:
Calories 440 • Protein 8g • Fat 7g (saturated 1g) • Carbohydrates 85g • Fiber 8g • Calories from fat 14% • Excellent source of vitamins A and C • Good source of folic acid

tomato and basil risotto

serves 4
preparation time: 10 minutes
cooking time: 20 minutes

once you know the secret to making a really good risotto it's easy to adapt the ingredients and change its identity completely. The important thing to remember is to add the liquid gradually to the rice. Once cooked, a good risotto should be slightly soupy, not mushy, and the rice should still have a little bite left in it. As with all risottos, keep the stock warm at all times; this way the rice will never stop cooking.

1½ cups (12¼ ozs.) fresh tomatoes
2½ cups vegetable stock (see page 62)
1 tablespoon olive oil
3 shallots, chopped
1¾ cups (14 ozs.) arborio rice
sea salt and freshly ground black pepper
1 large bunch of fresh basil leaves, roughly torn

❖ Put the tomatoes in a bowl, and cover with boiling water. After 20 seconds in the boiling water, plunge them straight into cold water. Drain and skin the tomatoes, then dice their flesh.

❖ Heat the stock in a saucepan until just simmering. It must continue to simmer while you cook the rice.

❖ Heat the oil in a large saucepan, and gently fry the shallots for 5 minutes, or until softened and golden. Add the rice, and stir for 2 minutes, until well coated. Add 2 ladles of stock and cook, stirring, until the rice has absorbed all the stock. Continue to cook, adding a few ladles of stock at a time, until all the stock has been absorbed and the rice is tender and creamy but still firm to the bite. If more liquid is required, use hot water.

❖ Remove the pan from the heat, season with salt and pepper, and stir in the fresh basil. Transfer to a warm serving dish, and serve immediately.

each serving contains:
Calories 430 • Protein 9g • Fat 6.5g (saturated 1g) • Carbohydrates 90g • Fiber 1g • Calories from fat 13%

caramelized fennel
and shallot risotto

serves 4
preparation time: 10 minutes
cooking time: 50 minutes

if you are fortunate enough to buy fennel bulbs that still have their feathery fronds attached, chop and scatter them over the risotto at the last minute along with the fresh tarragon. The tarragon enhances the fennel's aniselike flavor. I have added a little sugar to help speed up the caramelization process. However, if you prefer your risotto less sweet, leave out the sugar, and give the vegetables a little more cooking time to allow the shallots' natural sugars to caramelize.

4 cups vegetable stock (see page 62)
2 large fennel bulbs, about 1 lb. total
2 tablespoons olive oil
3 shallots, sliced
1 tablespoon light brown sugar, softened
1¾ cups (14 ozs.) arborio rice
sea salt and freshly ground black pepper
handful of fresh tarragon leaves, roughly chopped

❖ Heat the stock in a saucepan until just simmering. It must continue to simmer while you cook the risotto.

❖ Trim the tough stalks off the fennel bulbs. Shave off the bases, and remove any damaged outer layers. Slice each bulb in half lengthwise, cut out the core, and slice each half into thin strips.

❖ Heat the oil in a large saucepan. Add the fennel, shallots and sugar. Sauté gently for at least 30 minutes, until the vegetables caramelize and turn golden and sticky. Put in the rice, and stir for 2 minutes, until well coated. Add 2 ladles of stock and cook, stirring, until the rice has absorbed all the stock. Continue to cook, adding a few ladles of stock at a time until all the stock has been absorbed and the rice is tender and creamy but still firm to the bite. If more liquid is required, use hot water.

❖ Remove the pan from the heat, and season with salt and pepper. Transfer to a warm serving dish. Scatter fresh tarragon over the risotto, and serve at once.

each serving contains:
Calories 470 • Protein 9g • Fat 9g (saturated 2g) • Carbohydrates 93g • Fiber 3g • Calories from fat 18%

moroccan pilaf

serves 4
preparation time: 15 minutes
cooking time: 45 minutes

the great thing about this dish is that you can pop it in the oven and forget about it until the rice is cooked—just remember to set a timer, or you may come back to overcooked grains. I love the way Moroccans use citrus fruit and cinnamon in savory dishes. It makes a welcome change to dishes such as pilafs that can otherwise seem very similar.

2 tablespoons olive oil
$\frac{1}{2}$ cup (1$\frac{3}{4}$ ozs.) whole almonds, roughly chopped
1 large onion, chopped
2 carrots, diced
1 cinnamon stick
$\frac{1}{2}$ teaspoon ground cinnamon
approx. 1 cup (7 ozs.) long grain rice
$\frac{1}{3}$ cup (1$\frac{3}{4}$ ozs.) currants
$\frac{1}{4}$ cup (1$\frac{3}{4}$ ozs.) dried apricots
grated zest of 1 orange
$\frac{1}{4}$ teaspoon cayenne pepper
2$\frac{1}{2}$ cups water
sea salt and freshly ground black pepper

to serve
large handful of cilantro, roughly chopped
large handful of fresh chives, finely chopped

❖ Preheat the oven to 375°F. Heat the oil in a large flameproof casserole dish. Sauté the almonds over moderate heat for a few minutes, until golden. Add the onion, carrots and cinnamon, and sauté for 5 minutes, until the onion is soft and golden. Add the rice, and cook for 1 minute, stirring, to coat the grains. Stir in the currants, apricots, orange zest and cayenne pepper, and pour in the water. Season with salt and pepper, and bring to a boil.
❖ Transfer the casserole dish to the oven, cover, and cook for 40–45 minutes, until the liquid is absorbed and the rice is tender. Scatter fresh cilantro and chives over the pilaf, and serve.

each serving contains:
Calories 400 • Protein 8g • Fat 14g (saturated 2g) • Carbohydrates 62g • Fiber 3g • Calories from fat 33% • Good source of vitamins A and E

japanese rice bowl
with vegetables

serves 4
preparation time: 20 minutes, plus 15 minutes standing time
cooking time: 20 minutes

this is the classic Japanese way of preparing rice for sushi. It is slightly sticky and sweet, with a very subtle flavor from the rice wine vinegar and dashi-konbu, a type of seaweed. The dashi-konbu adds flavor to the rice as it cooks; it is available in sheets or pieces at Asian markets and some health food stores.

One 2″ x 2″ piece of dashi-konbu
1 cup (8 ozs.) Japanese sushi rice
2 cups (16 fl. ozs.) water
4 tablespoons rice wine vinegar
1 tablespoon turbinado sugar
pinch of sea salt
1 tablespoon vegetable oil
1½ cups (4 ozs.) shiitake mushrooms, sliced
1½ cups (4 ozs.) portobello mushrooms, sliced
2 carrots, thinly sliced
7 fl. ozs. vegetable stock (see page 62)
2 tablespoons soy sauce
1 tablespoon sugar
2 teaspoons corn flour
3 cups (6 ozs.) bean sprouts
2 cups (5½ ozs.) sugar snap peas
dark soy sauce, pickled ginger and wasabi

❖ Put the dashi-konbu and rice in a large saucepan with the water. Bring to a boil, and remove the dashi-konbu. Cover, and simmer the rice for 10 minutes. Remove from the heat.

❖ Stir 2 tablespoons of the vinegar, the sugar and salt in a small bowl until the sugar and salt have dissolved. Pour the mixture over the cooked rice. Cover, and set aside for 15 minutes.

❖ Heat the oil in a wok or deep frying pan. Add the shiitake and portobello mushrooms and carrots, and fry over moderate heat for 5 minutes, until lightly browned. Add the stock, soy sauce, remaining vinegar, sugar and corn flour. Bring to a simmer, and cook gently for 5 minutes, until the sauce is slightly thickened. Stir in the bean sprouts and sugar snap peas and cook for 1 minute.

❖ Transfer the rice to a warm serving dish. Spoon the vegetables over the rice, and serve with little bowls of soy sauce, pickled ginger and wasabi as accompaniments.

each serving contains:
Calories 315 • Protein 8g • Fat 4g (saturated 0.5g) • Carbohydrates 64g • Fiber 5g • Calories from fat 12% • Good source of vitamins A and C

spring vegetables
with saffron basmati rice

serves 4
preparation time: 15 minutes
cooking time: 20 minutes

this is a quick main course that looks as pretty and delicious as it tastes. Despite the few ingredients, the flavor is fabulous. There is something magical about saffron and the way it washes a golden hue over everything. A good way to maximize the flavor and color of the threads is to toast them in a metal spoon over low heat, then pound them using a pestle and mortar before steeping them in a few tablespoons of warm liquid. This kind of recipe extols the virtues of fresh vegetables. If you do not appreciate vegetables that have bite, you will need to cook them a little longer. I like to use baby vegetables, but if they are unavailable, larger ones will do just as well.

1½ cups (12¼ ozs.) basmati rice
2 medium-size tomatoes
large pinch of saffron threads
10 fl. ozs. hot vegetable stock (see page 62)
2 tablespoons olive oil
8 large spring onions, cut diagonally into thin slices
4 cups (14 ozs.) carrots, cut diagonally into thin slices
4 cups (14 ozs.) leeks, cut diagonally into thin slices
4 cups (14 ozs.) zucchini, cut diagonally into thin slices
sea salt and freshly ground black pepper
handful of fresh flat-leaf parsley, roughly chopped

❖ Bring a large saucepan of water to a boil, and add the rice. Bring back to a boil, reduce the heat, and simmer for 15–20 minutes, until the rice is tender. Drain, and keep warm.

❖ Meanwhile, put the tomatoes in a bowl, and cover with boiling water. After 20 seconds in the boiling water, plunge them straight into cold water. Drain and skin the tomatoes, then roughly chop the flesh. Put the saffron threads in a little bowl, and cover with 2 tablespoons of the vegetable stock. Let soak for 5 minutes.

❖ Heat the olive oil in a wok or deep frying pan, and sauté the spring onions over high heat for about 3 minutes, until soft. Add the carrots, leeks and zucchini, and cook for another 5 minutes, stirring occasionally. You may need to use 2 spoons to toss everything together. Stir in the tomatoes, the rest of the stock and the saffron and its liquid. Season with salt and pepper. Simmer for 3 minutes.

❖ Divide the rice among four warm bowls. Pile the vegetables on the rice using a slotted spoon, then drizzle their juices over the top. Scatter fresh parsley over them, and serve.

spicy vegetables
and coconut cream

serves 4
preparation time: 20 minutes
cooking time: 25 minutes

for maximum flavor, cook the spicy vegetables the night before, and keep them in the fridge. Reheat gently while you cook the rice. Coconut cream is very thick and creamy; you can find it canned and sometimes frozen in some supermarkets and Asian markets. Use unsweetened coconut milk instead if you prefer, but omit the water from the recipe.

2 lbs. mixed vegetables, such as broccoli, carrots, baby corn and tomatoes
2 tablespoons vegetable oil
1 large onion, sliced
2″ piece of fresh ginger, peeled and chopped
2 garlic cloves, crushed
1 lemon grass stick, thinly sliced
1 red chili pepper, seeded and finely chopped
2 teaspoons medium curry powder
sea salt and freshly ground black pepper
7 fl. ozs. coconut cream
1 cup (8 fl. ozs.) water
large handful of fresh basil leaves, roughly torn
large handful of cilantro, roughly chopped
1½ cups (12 ozs.) Thai jasmine rice

to serve
large handful of fresh basil leaves, roughly torn
large handful of cilantro, roughly chopped

❖ If using tomatoes, skin them (see page 46), then roughly chop their flesh. Cut the other vegetables into bite-size pieces.
❖ Heat the oil in a large saucepan. Add the onion, ginger, garlic and lemon grass, and sauté over moderate heat for 5 minutes, until softened. Stir in the chili pepper and curry powder, and season with salt and pepper. Cook for 5 minutes. Add the vegetables, and cook for 5 more minutes, then mix in the coconut cream and water. Simmer gently, covered, for 15 minutes. Mix the fresh basil and cilantro into the vegetables.

❖ Stir the rice into a large saucepan of boiling water, and simmer for 10–15 minutes, until tender. The rice should have a little bite left in it. Drain.

❖ Divide the rice among four warm bowls, and top with the vegetables. Scatter fresh basil and cilantro over the bowls, and serve.

each serving contains:
Calories 610 • Protein 15g • Fat 20g (saturated 11g) • Carbohydrates 93g • Fiber 6g • Calories from fat 30% • Excellent source of vitamins A and C • Good source of folic acid

juma's special african curry

serves 4
preparation time: 15 minutes
cooking time: 25 minutes

special thanks go to Juma Mashaka, the cook at Ras Kutani Hotel on the coast of East Africa where I sampled this dish. I have adapted it slightly, and this version is one of my favorites for four reasons: It is incredibly quick to prepare; you need only a few ingredients; you can use any vegetables that you happen to have available; and, last but by no means least, it brings back fond memories of my honeymoon. (Note: You should be able to find creamed coconut in Asian grocery stores.)

6 medium-size tomatoes
3 tablespoons sunflower oil
2 large onions, chopped
6 garlic cloves, finely chopped
1 orange pepper, seeded and coarsely chopped
2 tablespoons medium Madras curry powder
14 fl. ozs. canned unsweetened coconut milk
2 teaspoons creamed coconut
4 red chili peppers, seeded and chopped
8 cups (1½ lbs.) mixed fresh vegetables, such as
   carrots, sugar snap peas and baby corn
2 zucchini, sliced
grated zest of 1 large lime
1⅓ cups (10½ ozs.) basmati rice
handful of cilantro, roughly chopped
handful of fresh flat-leaf parsley, roughly chopped

❖ Put the tomatoes in a bowl, and cover with boiling water. After 20 seconds in the boiling water, plunge them straight into cold water. Drain and skin the tomatoes, then chop their flesh.

❖ Heat the oil in a large saucepan. Add the onions, garlic, orange pepper and curry powder. Cook, stirring often, for 5 minutes, or until the onion has started to soften. Stir in the tomatoes, coconut milk, creamed coconut and chili peppers. Bring to a boil, then reduce the heat, and simmer gently for 15 minutes.

❖ Meanwhile, prepare the mixed vegetables according to their type: If you are using large vegetables, chop them into bite-size pieces; leave small produce, such as sugar snap peas, whole. Add the mixed vegetables, zucchini and half the lime zest to the sauce, and continue to cook for 5 minutes.

❖ While the curry is simmering, bring a large saucepan of water to a boil. Add the rice, and cook for about 15 minutes, or until the grains are tender. Drain well. Mix the remaining lime zest with the cilantro and parsley.

❖ Divide the freshly cooked rice among four warm serving bowls, and spoon the curry on top. Scatter the lime zest and herb mixture over the top, and serve immediately.

each serving contains:
Calories 330 • Protein 8g • Fat 21g (saturated 10g) •
Carbohydrates 26g • Fiber 7g • Calories from fat 58% • Excellent
source of vitamins A, C and E

wontons with chili sauce

serves 4
preparation time: 25 minutes
cooking time: 10–12 minutes

if you can't find fresh shiitake mushrooms for this dish,
use dried porcini, and soak
them in warm water for 30
minutes before using. If rice
wine vinegar is unavailable, use
slightly less white wine vinegar
instead.

1 tablespoon vegetable oil
1½ cups (4 ozs.) portobello mushrooms, finely chopped
1 cup (2½ ozs.) shiitake mushrooms, finely chopped
2 spring onions, finely chopped
1 tablespoon soy sauce
1 tablespoon dry sherry
2 teaspoons sesame oil
pinch of sugar
pinch of salt
25 wonton wrappers
3–4 large lettuce leaves

for the chili sauce
4 tablespoons light soy sauce
2 tablespoons rice wine vinegar
1 tablespoon sesame oil
1 tablespoon hot chili sauce
1 garlic clove, crushed
4 spring onions, finely chopped

❖ Heat the oil in a frying pan. Add the portobello and
shiitake mushrooms and onions, and sauté over moderate heat for 5 minutes, until softened. Add the soy
sauce, sherry and sesame oil, and season with the
sugar and salt.

❖ Put 1 tablespoon of the mixture on the nonfloured
side of a wonton wrapper, moisten the edges with
water, and fold the wrapper over to form a little purse.
Pinch the edges together tightly to close. Repeat the

process until all the stuffing is used. You will probably fill about 20 wrappers.

❖ Line a heatproof plate with the lettuce leaves, and arrange the wontons on top in a single layer. Put a wooden or metal rack in a wok or wide pan, pour in 2 inches of water, and bring to a boil. Put the plate on the rack, cover, and steam for 6–7 minutes, or until the wontons are firm to the touch. While the wontons are cooking, put all the chili sauce ingredients in a screw-top jar and shake vigorously until well blended.

❖ Divide the wontons among four warm plates, and serve with the chili sauce as an accompaniment.

each serving contains:
Calories 130 • Protein 2.5g • Fat 8.5g (saturated 1g) •
Carbohydrates 10g • Fiber 1g • Calories from fat 60%

chilied spring rolls
with dipping sauce

makes 8 spring rolls
preparation time: 20 minutes
cooking time: 12–15 minutes

there may seem to be a lot of chili peppers here, but the hot seeds and membranes are removed in this recipe. The chili peppers are used in this recipe for their flavor. Remember to keep the filo pastry covered with a clean, damp cloth when you are not working with it to prevent it from drying out.

3 tablespoons pine nuts
8–10 green chili peppers
2 tablespoons vegetable oil, plus extra for brushing
2 bunches of spring onions, cut diagonally into thin slices
2 garlic cloves, chopped
1 tablespoon fresh ginger, grated and peeled
4 cups (8 ozs.) bean sprouts
2 teaspoons sesame oil
1 cup (8 ozs.) filo pastry, thawed if frozen

for the dipping sauce
(3½ fl. ozs.) soy sauce
1½" piece of fresh ginger, peeled and finely sliced
3 garlic cloves, crushed

❖ Preheat the oven to 350°F. Roast the pine nuts in a heavy frying pan over moderate heat, stirring frequently until golden. Seed the chili peppers, scraping away the membranes. Slice them finely.

❖ Heat the oil in a wok or large frying pan. Add the spring onions, garlic, chili peppers and ginger, and stir-fry over high heat for 5 minutes. Add the bean sprouts and pine nuts, and stir-fry for another 2 minutes. Add the sesame oil, and toss. Remove from the heat, and let cool.

❖ Spread out a sheet of filo pastry, and cut it in half. Cover the other half and the remaining sheets with a clean, damp cloth. Brush the pastry half with a little oil, and put 1 tablespoon of the filling in the center. Fold the sides over to enclose the filling, then roll the pastry over to form a spring roll. Brush the edges with a little oil, and press them firmly together to seal.

Place on a baking tray. Repeat with the remaining pastry and filling. Bake the spring rolls for 12–15 minutes, until golden and crisp.

❖ Put all the sauce ingredients in a screw-top jar, and shake vigorously until well blended. Serve the spring rolls with the sauce as an accompaniment.

each serving contains:
Calories 175 • Protein 4g • Fat 10g (saturated 1g) • Carbohydrates 17g • Fiber 1g • Calories from fat 53%

polenta with beans

serves 4
preparation time: 20 minutes
cooking time: 20 minutes

this recipe comes all the way from Ras Kutani, a beach resort in East Africa, which I found particularly stunning as I was on my honeymoon. Cornmeal (also known as polenta) and beans is the staple local diet—not a dish that appeared on the hotel menu. However, when I expressed an interest in their food, the staff was more than delighted to cook this dish and share it with us, on one condition: that we ate it with our hands! This is easier than it may seem. Take a piece of cornmeal, roll it into a ball, dip the ball into the beans, and enjoy. (I must confess I used a spoon towards the end—I didn't want to waste any of the delicious juices.)

2 tablespoons sunflower oil
1 large onion, finely chopped
2 teaspoons turmeric
7 fl. ozs. canned unsweetened coconut milk
10 fl. ozs. water
1¾ cups (14 ozs.) canned kidney beans, drained
1 cup (5½ ozs.) corn meal

❖ Heat the oil in a frying pan, and sauté the onions over high heat for 3 minutes, or until they soften and start to turn golden. Add the turmeric, and cook, stirring, for another 2 minutes. Stir in the coconut milk, and bring to a boil. Add the beans, and simmer for 10 minutes.

❖ Put the water in a large saucepan, and bring to a boil. Add the cornmeal by letting it run through your fingers in a thin stream while beating continuously over moderate heat. The cornmeal is cooked when the mixture leaves the sides of the pan.

❖ Pile the corn meal in a mound on a warm dish, and divide the beans among four warm bowls. Guests can have fun taking balls of the meal and dipping them into their beans. Alternatively, spoon a little pile of the cornmeal in the centers of 4 warm plates, top with the beans, and eat with a fork or spoon.

each serving contains:
Calories 350 • Protein 11g • Fat 12g (saturated 5g) • Carbohydrates 47g • Fiber 7g • Calories from fat 32% • Good source of vitamin E

sticky golden onion tarts

serves 4
preparation time: 20 minutes
cooking time: about 1 hour

to achieve really caramelized onions, always add any acidic liquids toward the end of cooking. The wine, vinegar and lemon juice will also help to counterbalance the sweet flavor of the onions. Be sure to use both a wine and a puff pastry that do not contain animal-derived products. Note: You may need to combine one sheet of puff pastry with some of another to get the 13 ounces specified in this recipe.

3 tablespoons olive oil
2 Spanish onions, sliced
2 leeks, cut diagonally into thin slices
1 red onion, cut into thin wedges
sea salt and freshly ground black pepper
5 fl. ozs. organic white wine
3 tablespoons white wine vinegar
1 tablespoon lemon juice
13 ozs. puff pastry, thawed if frozen
handful of fresh chives, finely chopped

❖ Preheat the oven to 375°F. Heat the oil in a saucepan or a frying pan with a lid. Add the Spanish onions, leeks and red onion, and stir until coated with the oil. Cover, and cook very slowly and gently for 1 hour. Season generously with salt and pepper. Increase the heat, and add the wine, vinegar and lemon juice. Stir until the wine has almost disappeared. Remove from the heat.

❖ While the onions are cooking, roll out the pastry on a floured surface, and use a saucer to cut out four 4″ circles. Prick the bases all over with a fork. When the onions have been cooking for about 40 minutes, put a baking tray in the oven for 1 minute to heat. Place the circles on the baking tray, and bake for 10–15 minutes, until golden and puffy. Turn the circles over, spoon some sticky caramelized onions on each one, and bake for an additional 5 minutes.

❖ Put the tarts on 4 warm plates. Scatter fresh chives over them, and serve.

each serving contains:
Calories 495 • Protein 7g • Fat 30g (saturated 1g) • Carbohydrates 44g • Fiber 2.5g • Calories from fat 56%

tuscan tarts

serves 4
preparation time: 20 minutes
cooking time: 20 minutes

I describe these tarts as Tuscan because they are packed with the wonderful ingredients so often associated with the region's cooking: olives, tomatoes, basil and peppers. You very often need only a few ingredients with their own fresh flavors to make a recipe a success. This is a classic example. Roasted peppers are available in jars and also at supermarket delicatessen counters. You may have to combine one sheet of puff pastry with part of a second sheet in order to get the required 14½ ounces for this recipe. Be sure to use a puff pastry that doesn't contain any animal-derived products.

1 cup (8 ozs.) ripe tomatoes
1 tablespoon olive oil
1 large onion, sliced
14½ ozs. puff pastry, from sheet, thawed if frozen
4 tablespoons good quality tapenade
About 1 cup (8 ozs.) jarred roasted peppers, drained
large handful of mixed black and green olives, pitted

to serve
extra virgin olive oil, for drizzling
handful of fresh flat-leaf parsley, finely chopped, *or* fresh basil leaves, roughly torn

❖ Preheat the oven to 400°F. Put the tomatoes in a bowl, and cover with boiling water. After 20 seconds in the boiling water, plunge them straight into cold water. Drain and peel the tomatoes, then quarter them. Set aside.
❖ Heat the oil in a frying pan. Sauté the onion over moderate heat for about 5 minutes, until soft and golden.
❖ Cut the pastry sheet into quarters, and place them on a baking tray. Spread 1 tablespoon of the tapenade over the middle of each quarter, leaving a border of about ½″. Cut the peppers into strips. Combine them with the tomatoes, sautéed onion and olives, and divide the mixture between the pastry quarters. Smooth it over the tapenade, making sure you don't cover the border.
❖ Bake for 15 minutes, or until the pastry is golden and puffy. Drizzle a little olive oil over the top, scatter the fresh parsley or basil over the tarts, and serve warm.

each serving contains:
Calories 390 • Protein 4.5g • Fat 30g (saturated 2.5g) • Carbohydrates 28g • Fiber 3g • Calories from fat 65% • Good source of vitamins A and C

malaysian vegetables

serves 4
preparation time: 10 minutes
cooking time: 10 minutes

cooking can-
not get simpler than this. This
dish is quick to prepare and
takes 10 minutes to cook. To
make the meal complete, serve
the vegetables with a bread of
your choice or a bowl of freshly
steamed rice.

5 plum tomatoes
2 tablespoons vegetable oil
1 Spanish onion, finely sliced
2 garlic cloves, finely chopped
1½ cups (4½ ozs.) snow peas
1 cup (4½ ozs.) frozen peas
6 baby carrots, quartered
1 teaspoon turmeric
1 teaspoon chili powder
14 fl. ozs. canned unsweetened coconut milk
3 cups (8 ozs.) Chinese cabbage, thinly sliced
sea salt and freshly ground black pepper
handful of cilantro, roughly chopped

❖ Put the tomatoes in a bowl, and cover with boiling
water. After 20 seconds in the boiling water, plunge
them straight into cold water. Drain and skin the
tomatoes, then cut them into bite-size chunks.
❖ Heat the oil in a wok or large frying pan. Add the onion
and garlic and sauté over moderate heat for 5 minutes,
or until softened. Add the snow peas, peas, carrots,
turmeric, chili powder and coconut milk. Simmer for 3
minutes, stirring constantly. Add the sliced cabbage and
tomato chunks, and simmer, stirring, for another 3 minutes. Season with salt and pepper.
❖ Divide the vegetables among four warm plates.
Scatter cilantro over them, and serve.

each serving contains:
Calories 235 • Protein 5g • Fat 16g (saturated 10g) • Carbohydrates 14g • Fiber 5g • Calories from fat 64% • Excellent source
of vitamins A and C • Good source of folic acid and vitamin B$_1$
(thiamin)

grilled vegetables on lemon grass sticks with coriander basmati

serves 4
preparation time: 30 minutes, plus 1 hour for marinating
cooking time: about 15 minutes

firm blades of aromatic lemon grass make novel, flavor-imparting skewers for these colorful grilled vegetables. Served with basmati rice tossed with cilantro chutney, they make a deliciously quick meal. Of course, you can always use wooden satay sticks instead of the lemon grass, and chopped fresh cilantro can be mixed with the rice instead of the chutney when you are in a real hurry. When warm weather is the inspiration for al fresco cooking, grill these little kebabs on the barbecue.

2 tablespoons peanut oil, plus extra for brushing vegetables
3 shallots, finely sliced
3 garlic cloves, roughly chopped
1″ piece of fresh ginger, peeled and roughly chopped
2 tablespoons soy sauce
juice of ½ orange
grated zest and juice of ½ lime
2 tablespoons turbinado sugar
1 teaspoon turmeric
1 teaspoon ground coriander
½ teaspoon cayenne pepper
1 tablespoon water
2 red peppers, seeded and cut into bite-size chunks
1 yellow pepper, seeded and cut into bite-size chunks
1 eggplant, cut into bite-size chunks
2 zucchini, cut into bite-size chunks
2 yellow zucchini or 4 pattypan squash, cut into bite-size chunks
8 lemon grass sticks, or wooden satay skewers, to cook
1½ cups (12¼ ozs.) basmati rice
handful of cilantro, roughly chopped

for the cilantro chutney
4 tablespoons (2 ozs.) cilantro, roughly chopped
1 tablespoon ground almonds
1″ piece of fresh ginger, peeled and roughly chopped
2 garlic cloves, peeled and roughly crushed
juice of ½ lime
2 red chili peppers, seeded and finely chopped
sea salt and freshly ground black pepper

❖ Heat the oil in a large frying pan or saucepan. Add and sauté the shallots, garlic and ginger over moderate heat for a few minutes, until golden.

❖ Stir in the soy sauce, orange juice, lime zest and juice, sugar, turmeric, ground coriander, cayenne pepper and 1 tablespoon water. Cook for a couple more minutes, then remove this marinade from the heat, and let cool.

❖ Add the prepared vegetables to the marinade, and toss everything together so that all the pieces are well coated. Cover, and set aside to marinate for at least 1 hour.

❖ Meanwhile, make the cilantro chutney: Mix the cilantro, almonds, ginger, garlic and lime juice with the chili peppers. Season with salt and pepper.

❖ Soak the lemon grass sticks or skewers in cold water for 10 minutes. Pierce a hole through the middle of each piece of vegetable, and thread the pieces onto the lemon grass sticks or skewers. Divide the vegetables equally between the sticks, alternating the pieces as you thread them on. Set aside while you preheat the grill on the hottest setting.

❖ Meanwhile, bring a large saucepan of water to a boil. Add the rice, and cook for about 15 minutes, or until the grains are tender. Drain well.

❖ While the rice is cooking, brush the vegetables with peanut oil, and grill for about 5 minutes. Baste the vegetables with any remaining marinade, turn them over, and cook for another 5 minutes.

❖ Fork half the cilantro chutney through the rice. Spoon the hot rice into 4 warm bowls or onto plates. Top each portion with a couple of vegetable skewers. Scatter cilantro over the top, and serve immediately, offering the remaining cilantro chutney as an accompaniment.

each serving contains:
Calories 475 • Protein 11g • Fat 9g (saturated 1.5g) • Carbohydrates 86g • Fiber 4g • Calories from fat 17% • Excellent source of folic acid and vitamins A, B$_1$ (thiamin), B$_3$ (niacin), B$_6$, C, and E • Good source of phosphorus

roasted vegetables with couscous and lemon pepper oil

serves 4
preparation time: 20 minutes
cooking time: 30 minutes

soaking the couscous as well as baking it makes the grains light and fluffy. Serve the roast garlic cloves whole so that everyone can squeeze the flesh out of the skins and enjoy the delicious flavor.

1 fennel bulb
12 medium-size vine-ripened tomatoes
2 red peppers, seeded and cut into bite-size chunks
2 zucchini, cut into bite-size chunks
1 red onion, cut into bite-size chunks
4 cloves garlic, unpeeled
4 tablespoons extra virgin olive oil
freshly ground black pepper
grated zest of 1 lemon
1 lb. couscous

to serve
large handful of cilantro, roughly chopped
4 lemon wedges

❖ Preheat the oven to 400°F. Trim the tough stalks off the fennel bulb. Shave off the base, and remove any damaged outer layers. Slice the bulb in half lengthwise, cut out the core, and slice each half into bite-size chunks. Skin the tomatoes (see page 46), then cut them into bite-size chunks.

❖ Put the fennel, tomatoes, peppers, zucchini, onion and garlic in an ovenproof dish. Drizzle 2 to 3 tablespoons of the oil over them. Scatter pepper and half the lemon zest over the top. Bake for 30 minutes, until slightly golden around the edges.

❖ Put the couscous in another ovenproof dish, and pour warm water over the top—just enough to cover the grains, but not flood them. Cover, and let sit for at least 10 minutes in a warm place. Fluff up the couscous grains with a fork. Add the remaining oil and lemon zest, and mix together. Cover the couscous with foil, and bake alongside the vegetables for 20 minutes.

❖ Mix the couscous and vegetables together, and scatter cilantro over them. Serve warm with lemon wedges and extra black pepper.

each serving contains:
Calories 425 • Protein 9g • Fat 13g (saturated 2g) • Carbohydrates 70g • Fiber 4.5g • Calories from fat 25% • Excellent source of vitamins A and C • Good source of vitamin E

potato cakes with peach and lemon grass chutney

serves 4
preparation time: 30 minutes
cooking time: 40 minutes, plus chilling time for the potato cakes; 1 1/2 hours for the chutney

there is something simply divine about these hot potato cakes served with a peach and lemon grass chutney. You will probably only use half the chutney with the cakes, so put the remainder in an airtight jar. It will keep for a few days in the fridge. If time is short, serve the potato cakes with a store-bought chutney of your choice. Alternatively, you could plan ahead and make the chutney when you have the time. Allow it to cool after cooking, and pour it into hot, sterilized jars. Seal, and store in a dark, cool place. Refrigerate once a jar has been opened.

for the chutney
2 teaspoons sunflower oil
3 lemon grass sticks, roughly chopped
1″ piece of fresh ginger, peeled and roughly chopped
2 large onions, roughly chopped
2 red chili peppers, seeded and chopped
2 teaspoons ground coriander
2 lbs. peaches, peeled, stoned and sliced
17 fl. ozs. white wine vinegar
1 cup (5 1/2 ozs.) light brown sugar, softened
1 cup (4 1/2 ozs.) currants
handful of cilantro, roughly chopped

1 lb., 10 ozs. potatoes, peeled
approx. 2 tablespoons extra virgin olive oil
sea salt and freshly ground black pepper
2 tablespoons vegetable oil
1 red chili pepper, seeded and finely sliced
1 large bunch of spring onions, finely sliced
large handful of cilantro, roughly chopped
4 slices white bread, crumbed
2 tablespoons paprika
vegetable oil, for shallow frying

❖ First, make the chutney: Heat the oil in a saucepan. Add the lemon grass, ginger, onions, chili peppers and ground coriander, and cook over moderate heat for 2 minutes. Reduce the heat to low. Add the peaches, vinegar, sugar and currants. Stir the mixture until the sugar has dissolved. Increase the temperature, and simmer gently for 1 1/2 hours, stirring occasionally, until the mixture is thick. Let cool. Add the cilantro, and mix well.

❖ Preheat the oven to 300°F. Line a plate or baking tray with paper towels. To make the potato cakes: Put the potatoes in a large saucepan of boiling water, and simmer for about 15 minutes, until tender. Drain. Return the potatoes to the saucepan, and dry them out over low heat, shaking the pan gently. Mash the potatoes with about 1 tablespoon of the olive oil, and season well with salt and pepper.

❖ Heat the vegetable oil in a wok or large frying pan, and sauté the chili pepper and spring onions over moderate heat for 5 minutes, or until soft. Spoon the spring onions onto the mashed potatoes. Add the cilantro, and mix well. Cover, and chill for 30 minutes.

❖ Shape the potato mixture into rounds, and brush with a little oil. Mix the bread crumbs with the paprika, and spread them out on a plate. Dip the potato cakes into the crumbs, turning and pressing them gently so that they are coated all over.

❖ Heat a thin layer of vegetable oil in a frying pan. Fry the potato cakes in batches over moderate heat for about 5 minutes, until golden all over. Drain the batches on the paper towels, and keep warm in the oven. Divide the potato cakes among four warm plates, and serve with big spoonfuls of peach and lemon grass chutney.

each serving contains:
Calories 645 • Protein 11g • Fat 13g (saturated 2g) •
Carbohydrates 129g • Fiber 7.5g • Calories from fat 19% • Good
source of vitamins C and E

moroccan spiced red potato
with chickpeas

serves 4
preparation time: 20 minutes
cooking time: 40 minutes

this very satisfying dish can quite happily be served on its own. However, it is also delicious on a bed of steamed couscous; the little grains absorb some of the Moroccan-flavored juices. You should be able to find harissa in Middle Eastern grocery stores.

2 red-skinned potatoes, unpeeled
1 lb. fresh ripe plum tomatoes *or* 1¾ cups (14 ozs.) canned chopped tomatoes
1 teaspoon cumin seeds
2 tablespoons olive oil
1 large onion, chopped
1 large garlic clove, chopped
large pinch of saffron threads
2″ piece of fresh ginger, peeled and chopped
1¾ cups (14½ ozs.) canned chickpeas, drained
1–2 teaspoons harissa
¾ cup (6 fl. ozs.) water
sea salt and freshly ground black pepper
handful of cilantro, roughly chopped
handful of fresh mint leaves, roughly chopped

❖ Put the potatoes in a small saucepan of boiling water, and simmer for about 20 minutes, until tender. Drain, and let cool. Cut the potatoes into cubes, leaving the skins on. Set aside. If you are using fresh tomatoes, skin them (see page 46), then roughly chop their flesh.

❖ Dry-fry the cumin seeds in a heavy frying pan over moderate heat, turning or stirring frequently, for a couple of minutes, until they start to pop and turn golden. Crush coarsely using a pestle and mortar.

❖ Heat the oil in a large saucepan. Add the onion, garlic, saffron, ginger and cumin and sauté over moderate heat for 5 minutes, until the onion is soft and golden. Stir in the tomatoes, diced potatoes, chickpeas and harissa, and pour in the water. Bring to a boil, then reduce the heat and simmer, covered, for 20 minutes. Season with salt and pepper.

❖ Transfer the potatoes to a warm serving dish, scatter cilantro and mint over them, and serve.

each serving contains:
Calories 270 • Protein 10g • Fat 9g (saturated 1g) • Carbohydrates 39g • Fiber 7g • Calories from fat 30% • Good source of vitamins C and E

mediterranean potatoes with olives, herbs and tomatoes

serves 4
preparation time: 15 minutes
cooking time: 55 minutes

these potatoes are visually appealing and very satisfying. All they need to accompany them is a fresh green salad dressed in a vinaigrette.

2 lbs. waxy potatoes, unpeeled
2 tablespoons olive oil
1 Spanish onion, finely sliced
1 clove garlic, chopped (optional)
sea salt and freshly ground black pepper
1 cup (7 ozs.) sun-dried tomatoes, cut into strips
1 cup (7 ozs.) mixed black and green olives, pitted
15 fl. ozs. vegetable stock (see page 62)
large handful of fresh flat-leaf parsley, roughly chopped

❖ Preheat the oven to 375°F. Bring a large saucepan of water to a boil, add the potatoes, and simmer for 10 minutes, until they are partly cooked. They should still be firm when pierced with a sharp knife. Drain.

❖ Heat the oil in a frying pan, and sauté the onion and sun-dried tomatoes over moderate heat for about 5 minutes, until soft and golden. Peel and thinly slice the potatoes. Oil an ovenproof dish. Arrange a layer of the sliced potatoes on the bottom, and season with chopped garlic, if desired, salt and pepper. Scatter some of the onion slices, tomato strips and olives over them, and season well. Arrange another layer of potato slices, then another layer of onions, tomatoes and olives. Continue the process until all the ingredients have been used, finishing with a layer of potatoes. Remember to season each layer.

❖ Bring the stock to a boil, and pour it over the vegetables. Bake in the oven for 30–40 minutes, until the potatoes are cooked and crispy. Scatter fresh parsley over the top, and serve.

each serving contains:
Calories 300 • Protein 6g • Fat 12g (saturated 2g) • Carbohydrates 43g • Fiber 5g • Excellent source of vitamin C • Good source of vitamins B$_1$ (thiamin) and B$_6$

eggplant and potato bake

serves 4
preparation time: 25 minutes
cooking time: 50–55 minutes

the eggplant's perfect, blemish-free purple skin never ceases to amaze me This vegetable always looks soft, glossy and perfect. The actual flavor of its flesh could be described as rather bland but, to me, that adds to its versatility. The soft flesh will absorb spices, chili peppers and garlic. And it can cope with strongly flavored ingredients such as chopped gherkin pickles, olives and fresh herbs. Serve this dish with fresh bread.

2 lbs. potatoes, peeled and cut into chunks
2 tablespoons extra virgin olive oil, plus extra for griddling and drizzling
3 large garlic cloves, crushed
sea salt and freshly ground black pepper
1 lb. ripe plum tomatoes
1 large eggplant, cut into thick slices

❖ Preheat the oven to 400°F. Bring a pan of water to a boil, and add the potatoes. Bring back to a boil, and simmer for 15-20 minutes, until tender. Drain, return the potatoes to the pan, and dry them out over low heat, shaking the pan gently. Add 2 tablespoons oil and the garlic, and season well with salt and pepper. Mash to a smooth puree.

❖ Put the tomatoes in a bowl, and cover with boiling water. After 20 seconds in the boiling water, plunge them straight into cold water. Drain, skin and seed the tomatoes, then roughly chop their flesh.

❖ Brush a griddle with a little olive oil, and heat until very hot. Put a few eggplant slices on the griddle, and cook for 5 minutes on each side, until golden and soft. Transfer to a shallow ovenproof serving dish. Repeat with the remaining eggplant slices. If you don't have a griddle, put the slices in the ovenproof dish, and cook in the oven for 10 minutes on each side.

❖ Spread the tomatoes over the eggplant, then spread the mashed potatoes over the tomatoes. Drizzle a little olive oil over the potatoes, and scatter salt and pepper over the top. Bake for 20-25 minutes, until golden and crispy and hot all the way through. Serve immediately.

each serving contains:
Calories 273 • Protein 6g • Fat 9g (saturated 1.5g) • Carbohydrates 43g • Fiber 5.5g • Calories from fat 30% • Excellent source of vitamin C • Good source of vitamin B$_1$ (thiamin) and folic acid

indian vegetables

serves 4
preparation time: 20 minutes
cooking time: 25 minutes

I must confess that when I ate this dish it was made with ghee (clarified butter). However, I was equally pleased with the end result when I developed a version using oil. As always, I have toasted the cumin seeds before crushing them to bring out their full flavor.

1 teaspoon cumin seeds
1 cup (7 ozs.) plum tomatoes or canned tomatoes
1½ cups (12¼ ozs.) basmati rice
1 tablespoon vegetable oil
1 large onion, sliced
3 garlic cloves, finely chopped
1 teaspoon turmeric
4 carrots, finely sliced
6 okra, halved lengthwise
¼ cabbage, shredded
1 cup (4½ ozs.) green beans, trimmed
2 green chili peppers, seeded and chopped
1″ piece of fresh ginger, peeled and grated
handful of cilantro, roughly chopped

❖ Dry-fry the cumin seeds in a heavy frying pan over moderate heat, turning or stirring frequently, for a couple of minutes, until they start to pop and turn golden. Crush coarsely using a pestle and mortar.

❖ If you are using fresh plum tomatoes, put them in a bowl, and cover with boiling water. After 20 seconds in the boiling water, plunge them straight into cold water. Drain and skin the tomatoes, then roughly chop their flesh.

❖ Bring a large saucepan of water to a boil, and add the rice. Bring back to a boil, reduce the heat, and simmer for 15–20 minutes, until the rice is tender. Drain.

❖ Meanwhile, heat the oil in a large frying pan. Sauté the onion over moderate heat for about 5 minutes, or until brown. Add the garlic, cumin seeds and turmeric. Fry, stirring, for another 2 minutes. Reduce the heat to low. Add the carrots, okra, cabbage and green beans, and cook, stirring, for another 5 minutes. Stir in the tomatoes, chili peppers, and ginger. Cover, and simmer for 10 minutes. The vegetables should be just tender. Scatter cilantro over them, and serve with the fluffy basmati rice.

each serving contains:
Calories 424 • Protein 11g • Fat 4.5g (saturated 0.5g) • Carbohydrates 84g • Fiber 7g • Calories from fat 10% • Excellent source of vitamins A and C • Good source of folic acid

balti

serves 4
preparation time: 15 minutes
cooking time: 10–12 minutes

I used to live in Henley-in-Arden, near the balti land of Birmingham, and it was there that I learned the basics of balti. As with all cooking, it is amazing what a difference it makes if you use whole spices and dry-fry them to bring out their flavor. Serve this balti with warm naan bread to mop up the juices. Be sure to pick ripe, juicy tomatoes.

5 medium-size vine-ripened tomatoes
1 teaspoon coriander seeds
½ teaspoon cumin seeds
½ teaspoon fennel seeds
6 whole green cardamoms
2 teaspoons fenugreek leaves
½ teaspoon freshly ground black pepper
½ teaspoon turmeric
3 tablespoons vegetable oil
½ cinnamon stick
3 garlic cloves, finely chopped
1 large onion, finely sliced
2 green chili peppers, seeded and sliced into rings
1 red pepper, seeded and roughly chopped
1 yellow pepper, seeded and roughly chopped
2 cups (5½ ozs.) portobello mushrooms, sliced
7 cups (14 ozs.) fresh spinach leaves
1¾ cups (14 ozs.) canned chickpeas, drained; reserve
   half the liquid
1 tablespoon mango chutney
sea salt and freshly ground black pepper

to serve
½ handful of fresh mint leaves, roughly chopped
½ handful of cilantro, roughly chopped

❖ Put the tomatoes in a bowl, and cover with boiling water. After 20 seconds in the boiling water, plunge them straight into cold water. Drain and skin the tomatoes, then roughly chop their flesh.
❖ Dry-fry the coriander, cumin and fennel seeds, cardamom and fenugreek leaves in a heavy frying pan over moderate heat, turning or stirring frequently, for

about 1 minute. Let cool, then crush coarsely using a pestle and mortar. Add the pepper and turmeric, and mix well.

❖ Heat the oil in a wok or large frying pan. Add the spice mixture, cinnamon stick, garlic and onion, and fry over moderate heat for 5 minutes, stirring constantly. Increase the heat, add the chili peppers, red and yellow peppers and mushrooms, and stir-fry for 3 minutes. Add the spinach and tomatoes, and stir-fry for another 3 minutes. Add the chickpeas and their reserved liquid and the mango chutney. Add more water if the vegetables seem to be drying out. Stir-fry for 2–3 minutes, then season with salt and pepper.

❖ Divide the balti among four warm plates. Scatter fresh mint and cilantro over the top, and serve.

each serving contains:
Calories 285 • Protein 13g • Fat 13g (saturated 1.5g) •
Carbohydrates 31g • Fiber 9g • Calories from fat 41% • Excellent
source of vitamins A, C and E • Good source of folic acid

stir-fried black beans
with lime and chili

serves 4
preparation time: 15 minutes
cooking time: 20 minutes

warm tortillas can hold many fillings and are always great fun to serve to friends. Provide a pile of warm tortillas, a bowl of hot beans and a dish of lime chunks, then leave everyone to help themselves.

8 tortillas
1 teaspoon cumin seeds
1 tablespoon vegetable oil
2 red onions, sliced into rings
2 garlic cloves, thinly sliced
1 teaspoon ground coriander
1/2–1 teaspoon chili powder
5 fl. ozs. vegetable stock (see page 62)
4 cups canned black beans, drained
juice of 1/2 lime
sea salt and freshly ground black pepper

to serve
large handful of cilantro, roughly chopped
4 wedges fresh lime

❖ Preheat the oven to 325°F. Wrap the tortillas in aluminium foil, and warm them through in the oven for 10 minutes.

❖ Dry-fry the cumin seeds in a heavy frying pan over moderate heat, turning or stirring frequently, for a couple of minutes, until the seeds start to pop and turn golden. Crush coarsely using a pestle and mortar.

❖ Heat the oil in a wok or large frying pan. Sauté the onions over moderate heat for 5 minutes, until soft and starting to turn golden. Add the garlic, ground coriander, crushed cumin and chili powder, and cook, stirring, for another 3 minutes. Pour in the stock, and simmer for about 10 minutes, until the liquid is reduced by half. Add the beans, and heat them

through. Stir in the lime juice, and season with salt
and pepper.
❖ Divide the beans among four warm bowls, and scatter
cilantro over them. Serve with the warm tortillas and
wedges of lime.

each serving contains:
Calories 540 • Protein 23g • Fat 5g (saturated 0.5g) •
Carbohydrates 105g • Fiber 16g • Calories from fat 9% • Good
source of vitamin B_1 (thiamin)

thai green vegetable curry

serves 4
preparation time: 20 minutes
cooking time: 15 minutes

you will only need 2 tablespoons of curry paste for this dish, but the paste will keep for a week in the fridge, so you can use it for other dishes such as Thai Pumpkin and Coconut Soup (see page 52).

for the thai curry paste
5 green chili peppers, seeded and roughly chopped
1½ lemon grass sticks, thinly sliced
2 tablespoons roughly chopped cilantro
1 teaspoon cumin seeds
1″ piece of fresh ginger, peeled and roughly chopped
3 spring onions, roughly chopped
2 garlic cloves, roughly chopped
1 teaspoon black peppercorns
½ teaspoon ground cinnamon
grated zest and juice of ½ lime

1 cup (8 ozs.) Thai jasmine rice
14 fl. ozs. canned unsweetened coconut milk
7 fl. ozs. vegetable stock (see page 62)
2 tablespoons Thai curry paste
pinch of sea salt
5 kaffir lime leaves
3 cups (8 ozs.) sugar snap peas, halved lengthwise
3 cups (8 ozs.) baby corn, halved lengthwise
2 cups (8 ozs.) small peas
1 red pepper, seeded and thinly sliced
1 orange pepper, seeded and thinly sliced
handful of fresh basil leaves, roughly torn

❖ First, make the Thai curry paste: Put all the ingredients in a food processor, and process until smooth. Set aside.
❖ Stir the rice into a large saucepan of boiling water, and simmer for 10-15 minutes, until cooked. The rice should have a little bite left in it. Drain.

❖ Meanwhile, bring the coconut milk and vegetable stock to a boil in another saucepan. Stir in Thai curry paste (store the remainder in a screw-top jar), and add the salt and lime leaves. Add the sugar snap peas, baby corn, small peas and red and orange peppers, and simmer, covered, for 10 minutes. Spoon the light fluffy rice into 4 warm serving bowls. Spoon the vegetable curry onto the rice. Scatter fresh basil over the top, and serve.

each serving contains:
Calories 405 • Protein 12g • Fat 11g (saturated 9g) •
Carbohydrates 60g • Fiber 6.5g • Calories from fat 26% • Excellent
source of vitamins A and C

eggplant butter with sea salt–crusted potatoes

serves 4
preparation time: 15 minutes
cooking time: about 1 hour

this thick, chunky puree is packed with flavor and is incredibly filling. It can also be served on top of baked potatoes or with thick, fresh bread and a green salad.

4 medium-size eggplants
6 fat garlic cloves
6 tablespoons extra virgin olive oil
4 large Idaho or russet potatoes
sea salt for the potatoes, plus extra for seasoning
2 teaspoons cumin seeds
3 tablespoons tahini
juice of 1 lime
large handful of cilantro, roughly chopped
freshly ground black pepper

❖ Preheat the oven to 425°F. Put the whole eggplants and garlic cloves on a baking tray. Coat the eggplant and garlic with 2 tablespoons of the olive oil.

❖ Put the potatoes on another baking tray. Coat them with 2 tablespoons of the olive oil, and scatter salt to taste over them.

❖ Put both baking trays in the oven, and bake for about 50 minutes, until the eggplant has softened and collapsed. Remove the eggplant from the oven. Bake the potatoes for an additional 10–15 minutes, depending on their size. When the eggplants have cooled a little, peel them and the garlic, and put the flesh in a sieve to finish cooling.

❖ Dry-fry the cumin seeds in a heavy frying pan over moderate heat, turning or stirring frequently, for a couple of minutes, until they start to pop and turn golden. Crush coarsely using a pestle and mortar.

❖ Put the eggplant and garlic, cumin, tahini, lime juice and remaining olive oil in a food processor, and process to a puree. Put the puree in a bowl, mix in half the cilantro, and season to taste with salt and pepper. Halve the potatoes lengthwise, and spoon some eggplant butter onto each half. Scatter the remaining cilantro over the top, and serve.

each serving contains:
Calories 450 • Protein 10g • Fat 25g (saturated 3.5g) •
Carbohydrates 50g • Fiber 10g • Calories from fat 50% • Excellent
source of vitamin C • Good source of folic acid and vitamins B_1
(thiamin) and B_6

eggplant slices
with lemon and cilantro

serves 4
preparation time: 10 minutes
cooking time: 40 minutes

whenever

I eat this, I seem to end up with eggplant and lemon juices dribbling down my chin. It is a meal in itself when served with fresh bread to mop up the juices.

3 large eggplants
4 garlic cloves, unpeeled
5 tablespoons extra virgin olive oil

to serve
large handful of cilantro, roughly chopped
freshly ground black pepper
2 lemons, cut into chunks

❖ Preheat the oven to 400°F. Slice each eggplant in half lengthwise, then slice each half horizontally. Make half a dozen deep diagonal slashes across each flat side, almost, but not quite, cutting through to the skin. Repeat at the opposite angle to produce a diamond effect. This will allow the heat to penetrate, and the eggplant will cook more quickly.

❖ Put the eggplant halves skin-side down in a roasting tin. Add the garlic, and drizzle 3 tablespoons of the olive oil over the top. Bake for 40 minutes, until the eggplant is soft to the touch but still retains its shape.

❖ Drizzle the remaining olive oil over the eggplant, and scatter cilantro on top. Serve warm with lots of freshly ground black pepper and chunks of lemon for squeezing.

each serving contains:
Calories 160 • Protein 2g • Fat 14g (saturated 2g) • Carbohydrates 5g • Fiber 4.5g • Calories from fat 84%

new potatoes and small peas
with pungent green sauce

serves 4
preparation time: 15 minutes
cooking time: 20 minutes

every time I go to Spain I eat a big selection of tapas, which always includes a sauce reminiscent of the one in this recipe. It is also fabulous tossed over fresh vegetables or as a dip for crunchy vegetables. Serve the potatoes with crusty bread and a salad.

4 garlic cloves
handful of cilantro
1 green pepper, seeded and coarsely chopped
½ cup (4 fl. ozs.) olive oil
2 tablespoons red wine vinegar
sea salt and freshly ground black pepper
1 lb., 10 ozs. new potatoes, unpeeled
1 cup (7 ozs.) small peas

❖ Put the garlic and cilantro in a food processor, and process to a paste. Add the green pepper, oil and vinegar to the paste, and process until smooth. Transfer to a bowl, and season with salt and pepper. Cover, and set aside.
❖ Put the potatoes in a large saucepan of boiling water, and simmer for about 15 minutes, until they are almost cooked but still just firm in the center when pierced with a sharp knife. Add the peas, and continue to simmer for about 5 minutes more, until the potatoes are tender. Drain.
❖ Transfer the potatoes and peas to a warm serving bowl, add the green sauce, and coat well. Serve warm.

each serving contains:
Calories 390 • Protein 8g • Fat 23g (saturated 3g) • Carbohydrates 41g • Fiber 5g • Calories from fat 53% • Good source of vitamins A and C

pacific rim coconut curry

serves 4
preparation time: 20 minutes
cooking time: 50 minutes

this is a filling little number, perfect to serve to burly young men. I speak from experience. My brother and his friends adore this curry and don't complain of being hungry when they've eaten it—which is often the case, even when I serve them meat. I use store-bought pastes very rarely; I always think it pays to toss fresh ingredients in a food processor and make my own base to a curry. So for a taste of flavors from the Pacific Rim— fresh root ginger, chili and garlic—get your food processor out, and start whizzing. Serve the curry with rice or chunks of fresh bread.

for the paste
2–3 tablespoons (1 oz.) cilantro
2 garlic cloves, finely chopped
1″ piece of fresh ginger, peeled and finely chopped
1 red chili pepper, seeded and finely chopped
1 green chili pepper, seeded and finely chopped
1 teaspoon light brown sugar, softened
1 tablespoon olive oil
2 tablespoons water
sea salt and freshly ground black pepper

handful of coconut shavings or dried coconut
4 medium-size vine-ripened tomatoes
3 tablespoons olive oil
2 large eggplants, about 1½ lbs. total, cut into large chunks
1 large onion, sliced
2¼ cups (12¼ ozs.) potatoes, peeled and diced
14 fl. ozs. canned unsweetened coconut milk
2 kaffir lime leaves or juice of 1 lime
10 fl. ozs. boiling water

❖ To make the paste: Put all the ingredients except the salt and pepper in a food processor, and process until smooth. Put in a bowl, and season with salt and pepper. Set aside.
❖ Dry-fry the coconut shavings or dried coconut in a heavy frying pan over moderate heat, turning or stirring frequently, for a couple of minutes, until golden. Set aside.
❖ Put the tomatoes in a bowl, and cover with boiling water. After 20 seconds in the boiling water, plunge

them straight into cold water. Drain and skin the tomatoes, then roughly chop their flesh.

❖ Heat the olive oil in a wok or large frying pan. Fry the eggplant over high heat for about 10 minutes, until the chunks are brown all over. Don't panic—the chunks will soak up all the oil at first, but as they begin to brown they will start to release it. Add the onion, fry for 2 minutes, then add the paste. Reduce the heat, and fry gently for 10 minutes, stirring occasionally to prevent the vegetables from sticking to the bottom of the pan.

❖ Meanwhile, add the potatoes, coconut milk, lime leaves or lime juice and boiling water to the curry. Simmer, covered, for 25 minutes. Stir occasionally to prevent the curry from sticking. Add the tomatoes a couple of minutes before the end of cooking, and heat through for 1 minute.

❖ Put the curry in a warm serving bowl, scatter the toasted coconut shavings or dried coconut over the top, and serve.

each serving contains:
Calories 325 • Protein 4.5g • Fat 22g (saturated 11g) • Carbohydrates 26g • Fiber 6g • Calories from fat 61% • Excellent source of vitamin C

crispy polenta peppers
and zucchini with
balsamic vinegar

serves 4
preparation time: 20 minutes, plus marinating time
cooking time: 20 minutes

I enjoyed something similar to this in a restaurant and had a go at making it as soon as I got home. Here is my version. It really is a nice way of serving crunchy vegetables. Don't worry if the cornmeal (polenta) falls off the vegetables when you fry them—just serve any excess crumbs with the vegetables. Remember to cut all the vegetables into similar-size strips so that they cook evenly. Serve them with Chunky Tomato Chutney (see page 170) for dipping and a fresh green salad tossed in a light vinaigrette.

2 red peppers, seeded and cut into thick strips
2 orange peppers, seeded and cut into thick strips
2 zucchini, cut into thick strips
2 carrots, cut into thick strips
2 garlic cloves, crushed
2 tablespoons extra virgin olive oil
1 tablespoon balsamic vinegar
5 tablespoons fine cornmeal
pinch of paprika
sea salt and freshly ground black pepper
vegetable oil, for frying

❖ Put the peppers, zucchini, carrots and garlic in a bowl, and drizzle the olive oil and vinegar over them. Marinate for at least 30 minutes, stirring occasionally. Drain. Discard the marinade.

❖ Preheat the oven to 300°F. Line a plate or baking tray with paper towels. Mix the cornmeal and paprika in a bowl, and season lightly with salt and pepper. Heat $1/4''$ oil in a frying pan. Toss the vegetable strips in the polenta, and fry them in batches for 3–4 minutes, until golden and crispy. Drain each batch on the paper towels, and keep warm in the oven. Scoop out any excess polenta with a slotted spoon, and sprinkle the crumbs over the vegetables. Serve in a warm bowl.

each serving contains:
Calories 330 • Protein 4g • Fat 20g (saturated 3g) • Carbohydrates 24g • Fiber 4g • Calories from fat 65% • Excellent source of vitamins A and C

roasted red onions and wilted spinach with sweet potatoes

serves 4
preparation time: 20 minutes
cooking time: 1 1/4 hours

I am a fan of roasting or caramelizing onions. Their natural sugars turn into a golden caramel that is sweet, sticky and simply gorgeous. In this recipe, the dressing of balsamic vinegar cuts through the sweet onions and potatoes.

3 red onions, peeled and cut into thin wedges
approx. 2/3 cup extra virgin olive oil
3 1/2 fl. ozs. balsamic vinegar
sea salt and freshly ground black pepper
4 large sweet potatoes
olive oil, for frying
3 1/2 cups (7 ozs.) baby spinach leaves
balsamic vinegar, for drizzling

❖ Preheat the oven to 425°F. Put the onions into an ovenproof dish, and drizzle the olive oil and vinegar over them. Season with salt and pepper. Cover the dish tightly with a lid or aluminum foil. Pierce each potato a couple of times with a skewer. Put the onions and potatoes in the oven, and bake for 1 hour. Remove the potatoes. Remove the covering from the onions, and bake for another 15 minutes.

❖ Heat a little olive oil in a wok or large frying pan. Add the spinach, and cook over high heat for a couple of minutes, until wilted. Halve the potatoes lengthwise. Mix the spinach into the onions, divide the mixture between the potato halves, and season well with salt and pepper. Drizzle balsamic vinegar over the top, and serve.

each serving contains:
Calories 500 • Protein 5g • Fat 28g (saturated 4g) • Carbohydrates 59g • Fiber 8g • Calories from fat 52% • Excellent source of vitamins A, C and E

individual crispy porcini bakes

serves 4
preparation time: 20 minutes, plus 30 minutes standing time
cooking time: 25 minutes

if you are fortunate enough to have access to fresh porcini mushrooms, use them; they are a real joy. Admittedly, they fetch a premium price, but the consolation is that a little goes a long way. Porcini are among the wild mushrooms that dry well. Others worth trying are morels and shiitake. To make sure you get maximum flavor (and your money's worth), use the soaking liquor in a wonderful stock for soup, the base to a stew, or, as in this recipe, a sauce for pasta.

5 fl. ozs. hot water
½ cup (1 oz.) dried porcini mushrooms
2 tablespoons olive oil, plus extra for drizzling
5 shallots, sliced
4 garlic cloves, chopped
1 lb. portobello and/or button mushrooms, sliced
1½ cups (12 ozs.) penne pasta
1 cup (2 ozs.) fresh bread crumbs
¼ cup (1 oz.) pine nuts
handful of fresh thyme leaves, roughly chopped
sea salt and freshly ground black pepper

❖ Pour the hot water over the porcini, and let stand for 30 minutes. Drain, and finely chop the porcini. Squeeze out their juice with your hands, and reserve all the liquor.

❖ Heat the olive oil in a frying pan. Add the shallots and garlic, and sauté over moderate heat for a few minutes, until softened and golden. They must not brown. Add the portobello and/or button mushrooms, and cook for another 5 minutes. Stir in the porcini and their reserved liquor, and boil rapidly for 5 minutes, until syrupy.

❖ Bring a large saucepan of water to a boil, and cook the pasta according to the instructions on the package. Drain, and return the pasta to the saucepan. Add the mushrooms, and toss well. Season with salt and pepper to taste. Divide the pasta among four individual gratin dishes.

❖ Turn the grill to high. Spread the bread crumbs and pine nuts out on a baking tray, and toast for about 2 minutes. Mix with the thyme, and scatter the mixture over the pasta. Drizzle a little olive oil on top, and pop the dishes under the grill until the topping is golden. Serve immediately.

each serving contains:
Calories 480 • Protein 17g • Fat 13g (saturated 1g) •
Carbohydrates 78g • Fiber 5g • Calories from fat 25%

spicy vegetable rounds
with chunky tomato chutney

makes 12 vegetable rounds
preparation time: 20 minutes
cooking time: about 45 minutes

handheld

food is easy to eat, and there is always an element of fun associated with it. This recipe is for those times when you feel like something hot and nourishing on the run. The vegetable rounds can be prepared ahead of time and kept in the fridge, awaiting a quick, shallow fry. (If time allows, you could bake them in a hot oven for 20 minutes.) The best way to serve them is hot inside slices of fresh ciabatta, with plenty of the chunky tomato chutney between the bread and vegetables. Supply napkins—eating can get messy.

1 lb. zucchini
sea salt and freshly ground black pepper
2½ cups (13 ozs.) sweet potatoes, peeled and cut into
    chunks
1⅔ cups (10½ ozs.) carrots, grated
1 green chili pepper, seeded and finely chopped
1 spring onion, thinly sliced
2 pinches of cayenne pepper, plus extra to serve
plain flour, for coating
vegetable oil, for frying

for the chunky tomato chutney
3 medium-size ripe tomatoes
1 tablespoon olive oil
2 shallots, thinly sliced
2 garlic cloves, crushed
2 tablespoons balsamic vinegar
1 tablespoon sugar
sea salt and freshly ground black pepper
handful of fresh basil leaves, roughly torn

❖ Preheat the oven to 300°F. Line a plate or baking tray with paper towels. Grate the zucchini, and sprinkle with salt. Set aside for 30 minutes to draw out some of the juices, then pat dry.

❖ To make the chutney: Put the tomatoes in a bowl and cover with boiling water. After 20 seconds in the boiling water, plunge them straight into cold water. Drain and skin the tomatoes, then dice their flesh.

❖ Heat the oil in a frying pan, and gently fry the shallots for about 5 minutes, until softened and golden. Add the tomatoes and garlic. Raise the heat slightly, and cook for a few more minutes, until the tomatoes have released some of their juices. Stir in the vinegar and sugar, and season to taste with salt and pepper. Simmer, stirring frequently, for 3–4 minutes, until the tomatoes have softened and the liquid has reduced slightly. Remove from the heat, and set aside. When the chutney has cooled slightly, stir in the basil leaves.

❖ Bring a saucepan of water to a boil. Add the potatoes, and simmer for about 15 minutes, until tender. Drain, and return the saucepan to the heat. Dry the potatoes over very low heat, shaking gently, then mash them. In a large bowl, mix the potato mash with the zucchini, carrots, chili pepper and spring onion. Add a pinch of cayenne pepper, and season with salt and pepper. Using floured hands, shape the mixture into small balls. Flatten the balls slightly, and coat them very lightly with flour. Sprinkle with a pinch of cayenne pepper.

❖ Heat a $\frac{1}{2}''$ layer of oil in a heavy frying pan. Fry 4 vegetable rounds over moderate to high heat for about 4 minutes on each side, until golden. Drain on the paper towels, and keep warm in the oven. Repeat the process with the remaining rounds.

❖ Sprinkle a little cayenne pepper over the vegetable rounds, and serve immediately with the tomato chutney as an accompaniment.

each serving contains:
Calories 320 • Protein 4.5g • Fat 20.5g (saturated 2.5g) •
Carbohydrates 31g • Fiber 6g • Calories from fat 58% • Good
source of vitamins A, C and E

moroccan-style chickpeas with saffron rice

serves 4
preparation time: 20 minutes
cooking time: 20 minutes

I have always been attracted to Moroccan flavors—the combination of saffron, cinnamon and ginger is just exquisite. This is a really quick supper. The rice cooks merrily alongside the chickpeas so that everything is ready at the same time.

1½ cups (12¼ ozs.) basmati rice
large pinch of saffron threads
4 medium-size ripe tomatoes
4 tablespoons olive oil
¼ teaspoon paprika
¼ teaspoon cayenne pepper
¼ teaspoon ground ginger
¼ teaspoon cumin seeds, roughly crushed
1 cinnamon stick, broken in half
1 Spanish onion, grated
1 lb., 13 ozs. canned chickpeas, drained
½ handful of cilantro, coarsely chopped
½ handful of fresh mint, coarsely chopped
5 fl. ozs. water
sea salt and freshly ground black pepper

❖ Bring a large saucepan of water to a boil, and add the rice and saffron. Bring back to a boil, reduce the heat, and simmer for 15–20 minutes, until the rice is tender. Drain.

❖ Put the tomatoes in a bowl, and cover with boiling water. After 20 seconds in the boiling water, plunge them straight into cold water. Drain and skin the tomatoes, then roughly chop their flesh.

❖ Heat the oil in a wok or frying pan. Add the paprika, cayenne pepper, ginger, cumin seeds and cinnamon stick, and fry gently for 3–4 minutes to cook off the spice flavor. Add the onion, and sauté over moderate heat for 5 minutes, until soft and golden. Add the tomatoes, chickpeas, cilantro, mint and water. Simmer gently, covered, for 15 minutes. Season with salt and pepper.

❖ Divide the saffron rice among four warm serving plates. Pile the vegetables on top, and serve immediately.

each serving contains:
Calories 670 • Protein 22g • Fat 17g (saturated 2g) •
Carbohydrates 108g • Fiber 9g • Calories from fat 23%

vegan lasagna

serves 4
preparation time: 15 minutes
cooking time: about 50 minutes

this is probably the closest I am going to get to a traditional recipe in this book. However, there is a reason why dishes such as lasagna are always popular. They do work, and they are a joy to eat. My vegan version is made of layers of creamy sauce, freshly cooked soft pasta, fresh green spinach, mushroom, nutmeg and a vividly red tomato and garlic layer. Serve with chunks of fresh focaccia and little bowls of extra virgin olive oil to dip the bread in. The number of lasagna sheets you use will depend on the size of your ovenproof dish. Make sure the sheets are in even layers and that they don't overlap—if they do, they will not cook properly and will taste tough and "doughy."

3 tablespoons olive oil
¼ cup (1 oz.) plain flour
2 cups (1 pint) vegetable stock (see page 62)
sea salt and freshly ground black pepper
handful of fresh flat-leaf parsley, roughly chopped
1¼ cups (5½ ozs.) vegan cheese, grated
1 large onion, sliced
2 cups (5½ ozs.) button and/or portobello mushrooms, thinly sliced
7 cups (14 ozs.) fresh spinach, roughly chopped
pinch of grated fresh nutmeg
2 garlic cloves, crushed
2 tablespoons tomato puree
1 lb., 12 ozs. canned chopped tomatoes
10–12 lasagna sheets

❖ Preheat the oven to 400°F. Put 1 tablespoon olive oil and the flour and stock into a saucepan, and whisk continuously over a gentle heat for about 5 minutes, until thick and smooth. Season with salt and pepper, and stir in the parsley and 2½ ozs. of the cheese. Set aside.

❖ Heat 1 tablespoon olive oil in a wok or large frying pan. Add the onion and mushrooms, and sauté over moderate heat for 5 minutes, or until the onion is soft and golden. Add the spinach, and cook for a minute, until wilted. Season with salt, pepper and nutmeg. Set aside.

❖ Heat the remaining olive oil in a large frying pan. Add the garlic, and fry gently for 3 minutes. Add the tomato puree and tomatoes, and simmer gently for 10 minutes, until the mixture has reduced to a thick, vivid sauce.

❖ Lightly oil an ovenproof dish, and spread half the tomato sauce over the bottom. Cover with a layer of lasagna. Spread one-third of the white sauce on top of the lasagna, then spread half the spinach and mushroom sauce over the white sauce. Cover with a layer of lasagna. Repeat the process; you will end with a layer of lasagna topped with white sauce. Scatter the remaining cheese over the top, and bake for 25–30 minutes, until the topping is golden and bubbling. Serve immediately.

each serving contains:
Calories 550 • Protein 26g • Fat 29g (saturated 13g) • Carbohydrates 47g • Fiber 6g • Calories from fat 49% • Excellent source of vitamins A, C and E • Good source of Vitamin B_3 (niacin) and folic acid

homemade pizzas

serves 4
preparation time: 25 minutes, plus 1¼ hours for rising
cooking time: 8–10 minutes

there are many different ways of making pizza dough. This method is based on a recipe I learned from an Italian who convinced me that it is the best. There is something very therapeutic about kneading pizza dough, but if you are not convinced, put the toppings on ready-made pizza bases or focaccia bread. Italians do not believe in putting lots of different ingredients on one base—they just use a few good-quality ingredients. I've suggested two pizza toppings, but you could invent your own: caramelize onions and make an onion pizza, or use a mixture of artichoke hearts, fresh tomatoes and olives. The only restriction is your imagination.

7 fl. oz. tepid water
1 packet (2¼ teaspoons) active dry yeast, crumbled
½ teaspoon sugar
1 teaspoon salt
3¼ cups (1 lb., 2 ozs.) flour
3 tablespoons extra virgin olive oil

for tomato and wild arugula topping
approx. ⅔ cup (5½ ozs.) crushed tomatoes
sea salt
2 tablespoons extra virgin olive oil
large handful of arugula, roughly torn, or fresh basil leaves, roughly torn

for fresh garlic and rosemary topping
4 garlic cloves, sliced
4 sprigs of fresh rosemary
sea salt
3–4 tablespoons extra virgin olive oil

❖ Put the tepid water in a bowl. Stir in the yeast and sugar, and let it sit for a couple of minutes, until the yeast has dissolved. Mix the salt and flour in a large bowl, and make a well in the middle. Pour the yeast mixture into the well, and use a wooden spoon to gradually bring the flour into the liquid from around the edges. When most of the flour is mixed in, slowly drizzle the oil into the middle of the flour mixture. Continue mixing in the flour until it forms a dough that comes away from the sides of the bowl—you may find it easier to use your hands at this stage. Remove the dough from the bowl, and put it on a clean surface. Knead it with your fingers and the palms of your hands for about 10–15 minutes, until it is smooth, soft and silky.

❖ Put the dough in a clean bowl, and cover with plastic wrap. Let rise in a warm place for 1 hour, or until it has doubled in size. Knock the dough back, and divide it into 2 balls. Cover the balls, and let them rise for 10 minutes.

❖ Preheat the oven to 425°F. Shape each ball into a large circle about 9 inches in diameter. Bring up the edges of each circle, and pinch them to form a rim. Lightly oil 2 baking trays, and transfer the circles to them. Prick the centers of the circles all over with a fork.

❖ To make the tomato and wild arugula pizza: Spoon the crushed tomatoes onto a pizza base, sprinkle with salt, and drizzle the olive oil over the top. Bake for 10 minutes. Put the pizza under a hot grill for a few minutes if you want it to be more golden, then scatter the arugula or basil leaves over the top, and serve immediately.

❖ To make the fresh garlic and rosemary pizza: Scatter the garlic, rosemary and sea salt over a pizza base, and drizzle the olive oil over the top. Bake for 8–10 minutes. Put the pizza under a hot grill if you want it to be more golden, then serve immediately.

If you want to make sure that your pizzas have crispy bases, buy a pizza stone or tile, available from good kitchenware shops. You can use two ¼-oz. packets of Rapid Rise yeast instead of fresh yeast: Add it to the flour with the sugar and salt, and mix the water and oil in afterwards.

each serving contains:
Pizza with tomato and arugula: Calories 560 • Protein 15g • Fat 15g (saturated 2g) • Carbohydrates 96g • Fiber 4g • Calories from fat 25% • Good source of vitamin B₁ (thiamin)
Pizza with fresh garlic and rosemary: Calories 580 • Protein 15g • Fat 18g (saturated 2g) • Carbohydrates 96g • Fiber 4g • Calories from fat 8% • Good source of vitamin D

desserts

warm hazelnut scones
with fruit salsa

serves 4
preparation time: 15 minutes
cooking time: 15 minutes

there is nothing quite like fresh, hot scones straight from the oven—and you don't need cream or butter to make them tasty. A thick, fruity salsa is simply delicious, and the contrast of warm and cold is sublime.

1 cup (3½ ozs.) hazelnuts
2 cups (8 ozs.) plain flour
3 tablespoons (1½ ozs.) vegan margarine
1½ tablespoons light brown sugar, softened
pinch of salt
5 fl. ozs. soy milk

for the fruit salsa
1 cup (8 ozs.) raspberries
grated zest and juice of 1 lime

❖ Preheat the oven to 425°F, and grease a baking sheet. Coarsely chop the hazelnuts. Roast them in a heavy frying pan over moderate heat, turning or stirring frequently, for a couple of minutes, or until golden.

❖ Sift the flour into a bowl, and rub in the margarine using your fingertips. Stir in the sugar and salt, then use a knife to gradually mix in the milk. Use your hands to lightly knead the mixture into a soft dough, adding a drop more milk if the mixture feels too dry.

❖ Turn the dough out onto a floured surface, and roll it out to about ¾″ thick. Use a 2″ round cutter to cut out about 15 scones, and place them on the baking sheet.

❖ Bake the scones for 12–15 minutes, until well risen and golden brown. Mash the raspberries with the lime juice while the scones are baking.

❖ Break open the hot, freshly baked scones, and spoon the salsa inside. Sprinkle a little zest over the fruit, and sandwich the scones back together. Devour!

each serving contains:
Calories 470 • Protein 10g • Fat 26g (saturated 1.5g) • Carbohydrates 50g • Fiber 5g • Calories from fat 51% • Excellent source of vitamins C and E

coconut rice pudding
with mango and papaya

serves 4
preparation time: 15 minutes
cooking time: 15–20 minutes

there's a taste of the tropics in every mouthful of this dessert. It looks stunning and tastes as indulgent as any rice pudding, but without the fat! Save the papaya seeds, and use them in a salad dressing—they are peppery and very good for digestion.

⅔ cup (5½ ozs.) jasmine rice
8½ fl. ozs. soy milk
8½ fl. ozs. canned unsweetened coconut milk
½ teaspoon vanilla extract
3½ fl. ozs. water
3 tablespoons (1 oz.) turbinado sugar
1 large ripe mango
1 large ripe papaya
handful of fresh basil leaves, to decorate

❖ Put the rice, soy milk, coconut milk and vanilla extract in a saucepan with the water. Stir, then bring to a boil. Reduce the heat, and simmer for 15–20 minutes, until the rice is tender but still has a bite to it. (Stir frequently to prevent the mixture from sticking to the bottom.) If necessary, add a few tablespoons of water to loosen the mixture. Add the sugar, and mix well. Simmer for another minute.

❖ Peel the mango, and use a sharp knife to slice the flesh away from the stone. Cut the flesh lengthwise into thin slices. Slice the papaya in half, and scoop out the seeds with a teaspoon, then peel. Cut the flesh into thin slices.

❖ Divide the mango and papaya slices among four large plates, and arrange the rice pudding next to them. Scatter fresh basil over the top, and serve.

each serving contains:
Calories 295 • Protein 5g • Fat 9g (saturated 6g) • Carbohydrates 50g • Fiber 2g • Calories from fat 27% • Excellent source of vitamin C

moroccan spiced rice pudding

serves 4
preparation time: 15 minutes
cooking time: about 25 minutes

ingredients

such almonds and dried fruit play a major role in Moroccan desserts. I love the combination of almonds, apricots and raisins, especially with the addition of a splash of orange-flower water (available at supermarkets).

4 cups (2 pints) soy milk
3½-5 tablespoons (1¾–2½ ozs.) jasmine rice
2 tablespoons rice flour
1 cup (6 ozs.) turbinado sugar
1¼ cups (4½ ozs.) ground almonds
½ handful of dried apricots, soaked in orange-flower water to cover
½ handful of raisins, soaked in orange-flower water to cover
¼ teaspoon almond extract
½ teaspoon vanilla extract
2 tablespoons orange-flower water
pinch of ground cinnamon, for dusting

❖ Put 3 cups (1½ pints) of the soy milk in a saucepan, and bring gently to a boil. Add the rice, reduce the heat, and simmer for 15–20 minutes, until the rice is tender but still has a bite to it. (Stir frequently to prevent the mixture sticking from to the bottom.) If necessary, add a few tablespoons of water to loosen the mixture.

❖ In a small bowl, mix the rice flour with about 2 tablespoons water—enough to make a smooth paste. Add the remaining milk to the paste, and stir well. Pour the rice flour mixture into the saucepan with the rice, and bring to a boil over low heat, stirring constantly. Add the sugar, ground almonds, apricots and raisins, and simmer gently, stirring constantly, until the mixture thickens. Remove the saucepan from the heat, and stir in the almond and vanilla extracts and the orange-flower water. Let cool for a few minutes.

❖ Divide the rice pudding among four short, fat drinking glasses, and chill in the fridge for several hours. Dust with ground cinnamon, and serve.

each serving contains:
Calories 560 • Protein 17g • Fat 23g (saturated 2g) • Carbo-hydrates 73g • Fiber 3g • Calories from fat 37% • Excellent source of vitamin E • Good source of riboflavin and vitamin B$_2$

baked pears and ginger

serves 6
preparation time: 10 minutes
cooking time: 20–30 minutes

pears are often poached, but rarely baked. These pears taste delicious served with soy ice cream or a scoop of Coconut Ice (see page 193). For extra color, scatter a few fresh mint leaves over the top just before serving.

6 firm pears, such as Comice
juice of 1 lemon
1 rounded tablespoon turbinado sugar
1 teaspoon vanilla extract
4 pieces of sweet red candied ginger, packed in red ginger syrup, drained and thinly sliced
2 tablespoons ginger syrup from the sweet red candied ginger

❖ Preheat the oven to 400°F. Peel, halve and core the pears. Put them in a bowl, sprinkle the lemon juice over them, and toss until the pears are well coated. Arrange the pears, cut side up, in an ovenproof dish.

❖ Put the sugar, vanilla extract, candied ginger and ginger syrup in the bowl that contained the pears. Mix with any leftover lemon juice, and pour the mixture over the pears. Bake for 20–30 minutes, basting occasionally, until the pears are tender and golden at the edges. Serve warm or hot.

each serving contains:
Calories 90 • Protein 0.5g • Carbohydrates 22g • Fiber 4g

hot poached pears
with toffee crisps

serves 4
preparation time: 25 minutes
cooking time: 35 minutes

I only add sugar to fruit desserts if absolutely necessary. Fruit has its own natural sugar and is very often sweet enough. However, they may need a little help if they are underripe, so taste before deciding whether additional sugar is needed. Pears are a great source of vitamin C. I eat a lot of fresh grapes and use grape juice in cooking. Grapes have been revered for many years as the queen of fruit, because of their ability to cleanse and purify the body.

5 fl. ozs. grape juice
2 tablespoons turbinado sugar
4 ripe pears
handful of fresh mint leaves, roughly torn

for the toffee crisps
4 wheat tortillas, cut into 1″ strips
confectioners' sugar, for dusting

❖ Put the grape juice and sugar in a saucepan (preferably stainless steel or enamelled cast iron) large enough to hold 4 pears. Heat gently to dissolve the sugar, then bring to a simmer.

❖ Meanwhile, peel the pears. Use a vegetable peeler to peel them from top to bottom, in strips, so that the fruit is smooth. Slice off the bottoms of the pears so that they sit easily. Sit the pears in the grape juice, and simmer gently, frequently spooning the hot juice over the fruit, for about 30 minutes, until tender. Remove the pears, bring the syrup to a boil, and reduce by one-third.

❖ Meanwhile, make the toffee crisps: Preheat the grill to high. Place the tortilla strips on a baking tray, and grill for 1 minute, until beginning to brown. Dust heavily with the confectioners' sugar, and return to the grill for another few minutes, or until the sugar has caramelized.

❖ Divide the pears among four plates, and drizzle the syrup over them. Scatter fresh mint leaves over the the pears, and serve with the toffee crisps.

each serving contains:
Calories 305 • Protein 4g • Fat negligible • Carbohydrates 75g • Fiber 4.5g • Calories from fat 2.4%

poached fruit in lavender-infused syrup
with toffee crisps

serves 4
preparation time: 15 minutes
cooking time: 25 minutes

i love lavender's slightly aromatic flavor, especially in a light vanilla sugar syrup. The great thing about this recipe is that it can be made in advance and left to cool until needed—just pop the tortilla strips under the grill when you are nearly ready to eat. Like all food, the presentation is critical, so for a really stunning effect serve the fruit in wine glasses with a couple of toffee crisps at right angles to one another resting on the top of each glass.

¾ cup (4½ ozs.) turbinado sugar
10 fl. ozs. water
flowers from 3 sprigs of lavender
1 vanilla pod, split
6 apricots
5 peaches
5 fl. ozs. organic white wine
Toffee Crisps (see page 185)

❖ Put the sugar and water in a saucepan (preferably stainless steel or enamelled cast iron), and heat gently to dissolve the sugar. Bring to a boil, add the lavender flowers and vanilla pod, and simmer for 10 minutes.
❖ Peel, pit and halve the apricots and peaches, then cut them into quarters, and slide the pieces into the syrup. Simmer gently, until the fruit is tender. This will take about 5–10 minutes, depending on the ripeness of the fruit.
❖ Use a draining spoon to remove the fruit from the syrup, then divide the quarters among four glasses or dishes. Pour the wine into the syrup, and stir. Then strain the liquid onto the fruit, and chill in the fridge. Serve the chilled lavender-infused fruit with hot toffee crisps.

each serving contains:
Calories 200 • Protein 2g • Carbohydrates 46g • Fiber 3g •
Excellent source of vitamin C

fruit with
cardamom and vanilla

serves 4
preparation time: 15 minutes
cooking time: 15 minutes

this is an excellent example of how fresh, tasty and exciting vegan desserts can be. It is important to remember that the longer you leave the spices in the syrup, the spicier it becomes. This may sound obvious, but if you leave them for half a day, the syrup will probably be a little too strong for your guests. It can be served with or without the spices. Experiment with other fruit in season.

½ cup (2½ ozs.) turbinado sugar
4 fl. ozs. water
4 green cardamom pods
3 star anise
couple of drops of vanilla extract
4 black peppercorns
4 fl. ozs. orange juice
3 bananas
4 ripe peaches
1 cup (8 ozs.) blueberries

❖ Put the sugar and water in a saucepan (preferably stainless steel or enamelled cast iron), and heat gently until the the sugar has dissolved. Add the cardamom, star anise, vanilla extract, peppercorns and orange juice. Bring to a boil, and simmer gently, covered, for 10 minutes. Remove from the heat, and let cool.

❖ Peel the bananas, cut them diagonally into thick slices, and divide them among four large soup plates. Peel, stone and thinly slice the peaches. Scatter the peach slices and blueberries over the bananas, and drizzle the syrup over all. Serve.

each serving contains:
Calories 200 • Protein 2g • Fat less than 1g (none saturated) •
Carbohydrates 50g • Fiber 4g • Calories from fat 2% • Excellent
source of vitamin C

orange and passion fruit sorbet

serves 4
preparation time: 20 minutes, plus freezing time
cooking time: 5 minutes

I spent three years as a development chef for a company that produces ice creams and sorbets, and as a result I tend to be fussy when it comes to fruit sorbets or sherbets. To my mind, there are at least two important criteria by which to judge them.

First, a sorbet should taste of its ingredients—this may sound obvious, but it is fundamental and so often not the case. In this recipe, the strong passion fruit and orange flavor comes from using fresh fruit (which means a lot of oranges), rather than lots of water and very little fruit, to make the juice. Second, the texture must be smooth and creamy, not icy and crunchy. The best way to achieve this is to make the sorbet in an ice cream machine, which will freeze the mixture

4½ lbs. oranges
1½ cups (9 ozs.) turbinado sugar
10 passion fruit
handful of fresh mint leaves, roughly torn

❖ Slice the oranges in half horizontally, and scoop out the flesh with a tablespoon. Put the flesh in a sieve, and strain the juice into a large bowl, pressing the flesh firmly against the sieve. Put the juice in a saucepan (preferably stainless steel or enamelled cast iron), stir in the sugar, and heat gently for about 5 minutes, until the sugar has dissolved. Let cool.

❖ Slice 9 passion fruit in half horizontally, and scoop out the flesh with a teaspoon. Put the flesh in a jug, and set aside 12 of the shells. Strain the juice into a bowl, pressing the pulp firmly against the sieve. Stir the passion fruit juice into the orange syrup.

❖ Transfer the syrup to an ice cream machine, and freeze according to the manufacturer's instructions. Alternatively, pour the syrup into a freezer-proof container, cover, and freeze for 2 hours. Remove the container from the freezer, and beat the mixture vigorously with a fork or electric whisk to break down the ice crystals. Cover, return the sorbet to the freezer for an additional 2 hours, and repeat the process. Cover, return the sorbet to the freezer, and let it sit for 2–3 hours, until it hardens.

❖ Use a teaspoon to scoop the sorbet into the reserved passion fruit shells; put 3 shells on each of 4 plates. Slice the remaining passion fruit in half, and drizzle a little of its juice over the sorbets. Top each with fresh mint leaves, and serve. Keep the remaining sorbet covered in the freezer.

rapidly. If you don't have a machine, freeze the sorbet in a domestic freezer, but remember to beat the mixture vigorously at intervals with a fork or electric whisk while it freezes in order to break down the ice crystals.

each serving contains:
Calories 44 • Protein 6g • Carbohydrates 110g • Excellent source of vitamin C • Good source of folic acid

papaya and coconut sherbet

serves 4
preparation time: 20 minutes, plus freezing
cooking time: 10 minutes

I describe this dessert as a sherbet because the creamed coconut (available in Asian grocery stores) and coconut shavings create a totally different eating experience. Serve it with fresh coconut, grated ginger and rum for a complete tropical sensation.

1¼ cups (8 ozs.) turbinado sugar
7½ fl. ozs. water
4 ripe papaya, peeled, seeded and cut into chunks
½ cup (3 ozs.) creamed coconut
5 tablespoons rum, plus extra for drizzling
grated zest of ½ lime

to decorate
handful of fresh coconut shavings
freshly grated fresh ginger (optional)

❖ Put the sugar and water in a saucepan (preferably stainless steel or enamelled cast iron), and heat gently for 10 minutes, until the sugar has dissolved. Pour the syrup into a large bowl, and let cool.

❖ Put the papaya in a food processor, and process to a smooth puree. Stir the puree, creamed coconut, rum and lime zest into the syrup, and mix until smooth.

❖ Transfer the mixture to an ice cream machine, and freeze according to the manufacturer's instructions. Alternatively, pour it into a freeze-proof container, cover, and freeze for 2 hours. Remove the container from the freezer, and beat the mixture vigorously with a fork or electric whisk to break down the ice crystals. Cover, return the sherbet to the freezer for another hour, and repeat the process. Cover, and return the sherbet to the freezer for at least 2 hours, until it hardens.

❖ Dry-fry the coconut shavings in a heavy frying pan over moderate heat, turning or stirring frequently, for a couple of minutes, until just turning golden.

❖ Divide the sherbet among four tall glasses. Drizzle a little rum over each serving. Scatter the coconut shavings and freshly grated ginger, if using, over the top. Serve.

each serving contains:
Calories 405 • Protein 1.5g • Fat 7g (saturated 6g) • Carbohydrates 77g • Fiber 5g • Calories from fat 16% • Excellent source of vitamin C • Good source of vitamin A

coconut ice dessert
with chocolate sauce

serves 4
preparation time: 20 minutes, plus freezing time
cooking time: 5 minutes

although this is not technically an ice cream, it tastes just like one. I am proud of this recipe—it is always pleasing to achieve a fabulous flavor and texture without using cream and other dairy ingredients. I've paired it with a chocolate sauce here. If you wish, you could ripple the sauce through the frozen ice rather than serving it separately—but you could also serve the ice with chopped fresh mango and papaya. If you can find a fresh coconut, toast shavings of the flesh, and scatter them over it. And, of course, it's good on its own.

2 cups (1 pint) soy milk
1 vanilla pod, split
1½ cups (4½ ozs.) shredded coconut
2 tablespoons custard powder
¾ cup (4½ ozs.) turbinado sugar
14 fl. ozs. canned unsweetened coconut milk

for the chocolate sauce
2 heaping tablespoons cocoa powder
2 heaping tablespoons light brown sugar, softened
3 tablespoons corn syrup
4 fl. ozs. water

❖ Put the soy milk and vanilla pod in a saucepan, and bring to a boil. Turn the heat off, cover, and let the milk become infused with the vanilla.

❖ Dry-fry the shredded coconut in a heavy frying pan over moderate heat, turning or stirring frequently, for a few minutes, until golden.

❖ Meanwhile, put the custard powder and sugar in a small bowl. Add about 2 tablespoons of the hot milk, and mix to a paste. Stir the paste into the infused milk in the saucepan, and bring back to a boil, stirring constantly, for at least 5 minutes, or until the milk thickens. Add the coconut milk and shredded coconut, and stir well. Let cool.

❖ Transfer the mixture to an ice cream machine, and freeze according to the manufacturer's instructions. Alternatively, pour it into a freezer-proof container, cover, and freeze for 2 hours. Remove the container from the freezer, and beat the mixture vigorously with a fork or electric whisk to break down the ice crystals.

Cover, and return the mixture to the freezer for another 2 hours.

❖ To make the chocolate sauce: Put the cocoa powder, sugar, corn syrup and water in a saucepan, and heat gently until the cocoa and sugar have dissolved. Bring to a boil, then reduce the heat, and simmer gently for 2–3 minutes, until thick.

❖ Divide the coconut ice among four bowls or glasses, and serve the hot chocolate sauce as an accompaniment.

each serving contains:
Calories 495 • Protein 6g • Fat 26g (saturated 20g) •
Carbohydrates 59g • Fiber 3g • Calories from fat 47%

lemon sherbet cups with crushed blueberries

serves 4
preparation time: 20 minutes, plus freezing time
cooking time: 5 minutes

the combination of lemon sherbet and crushed blueberries makes a refreshing dessert. Alternatively, serve the sherbet on its own to cleanse the palate between courses. There is a higher than usual proportion of water in the sherbet, because the flavor of the lemons would otherwise be too intense.

3 large lemons, washed, plus 1 tablespoon lemon juice
1 cup (6½ ozs.) turbinado sugar, plus 1 teaspoon
9 fl. ozs. water
1¼ cups (8½ ozs.) blueberries

❖ Peel the zest from 1 lemon, and squeeze out its juice. Carefully cut the remaining lemons in half horizontally, and squeeze out their juice. Reserve the halves. In a large saucepan (preferably stainless steel or enamelled cast iron), mix the lemon zest, juice of all 3 lemons and sugar with the water. Heat gently for 5 minutes, until the sugar has dissolved.

❖ Transfer the mixture to an ice cream machine, and freeze according to the manufacturer's instructions. Alternatively, pour it into a freezer-proof container, cover, and freeze for 2 hours. Remove the container from the freezer, and beat the mixture vigorously with a fork or electric whisk to break down the ice crystals. Cover, return the sherbet to the freezer, leave for another hour, and repeat the process. Cover, and return the sherbet to the freezer for at least 2 hours, until it hardens.

❖ Crush the blueberries, and mix them with 1 tablespoon lemon juice and 1 teaspoon sugar (or to taste). Divide the sherbet between the lemon halves. Drizzle the crushed blueberries over the center of each one, and serve.

each serving contains:
Calories 200 • Protein 0.5g • Carbohydrates 52g • Fiber 2g •
Excellent source of vitamin C

frozen yogurt crunch with raspberry sauce

serves 4
preparation time: 20 minutes

this may seem childish, but adults love this dessert as much as children. Make it, and keep it in the freezer until you fancy a sweet fix. I developed this recipe one day when I put some biscuits and jam in the freezer—I am a firm believer that most creations happen when you least expect them to. I have used gingersnaps here, but any sweet biscuits will do. Just check the label to make sure they are vegan. Similarly, the frozen yogurt can be replaced by soy ice cream.

approx. 1¼ cups (9 ozs.) crunchy cereal
approx. ⅔ cup (5½ ozs.) gingersnaps
3 tablespoons low-sugar fruit jam
approx. 1⅓ cups (10½ ozs.) frozen vanilla soy yogurt
1¼ cups (9 ozs.) raspberries
dash of lime juice
1 teaspoon confectioners' sugar

❖ Finely crush the cereal and gingersnaps with a rolling pin, then mix the crumbs with the jam. Spoon the mixture into 24 paper mini muffin cups, and press it down firmly. Fill the cups with the frozen yogurt, and cover them with foil or plastic wrap. Arrange the cups on a baking tray, and freeze for 20 minutes.

❖ Push the raspberries through a sieve with a wooden spoon. Stir in the lime juice and confectioners' sugar. Serve the yogurt crunch with a jug of raspberry sauce for drizzling over them.

each serving contains:
Calories 565 • Protein 9g • Fat 17g (saturated 5.5g) •
Carbohydrates 96g • Fiber 12g • Calories from fat 28% • Good
source of vitamin C

fresh fruit in wine with basil

serves 4
preparation time: 20 minutes

for a really light and dazzling dessert, serve the fruit in wine glasses with just enough wine to cover them. Fresh basil has a wonderfully sweet and subtle flavor—I often scatter it over a plate of fresh strawberries or other soft fruit for a very simple, elegant dessert. The amount of wine you use will depend on the size of your glasses—you may not need the whole bottle.

1 large ripe mango
1 large ripe papaya
1 lb. strawberries, hulled and sliced
2 bananas, peeled and sliced
4 apricots, stoned and sliced
1 bottle organic white wine
handful of fresh basil leaves

❖ Peel the mango, and use a sharp knife to slice the flesh away from the stone. Cut the flesh into thin slices about 2 inches long, and put it in a bowl. Slice the papaya in half lengthwise, scoop out the seeds with a teaspoon, and peel. Cut the flesh into thin slices about 2 inches long, and add them to the mango. Add the strawberries, bananas and apricots, and mix well.

❖ Divide the fruit among four wine glasses. Pour enough wine over them to cover. Scatter fresh basil on top, and serve.

each serving contains:
Calories 250 • Protein 2.5g • Carbohydrates 30g • Fiber 4g •
Excellent source of vitamin C

strawberries with black pepper

serves 4
preparation time: 20 minutes

the simplicity of this dessert appeals to me. It may seem a strange combination, but the pepper really enhances the fruity strawberry flavor. Use fresh strawberries when they are in season. Better still are wild strawberries, which are bursting with 10 times more flavor than the large ones grown commercially.

1 lb. strawberries, hulled and thinly sliced
3 blood oranges
freshly ground black pepper

❖ Arrange the strawberries in a single layer on 4 plates. Peel 2 of the oranges with a sharp knife, making sure you remove all the white pith, then cut the flesh into thin slices. Arrange the orange slices in between the strawberries so that you can see both fruits. Cut the remaining orange in half, and squeeze the juice over the fruit. Grind a sprinkling of pepper over each serving.

each serving contains:
Calories 78 • Protein 2g • Carbohydrates 17g • Fiber 3g • Excellent source of vitamin C

toffee figs
with a glass of brandy

serves 4
preparation time: 20 minutes
cooking time: 20 minutes

to me, fresh figs are one of the most sensual fruits in the world. Choose ones that are soft to the touch with a fruity (not sour) smell. Figs are sometimes criticized for their lack of sweetness, which may be why they are often turned into fig puddings or biscuits. Any sceptics should give these figs a go—encased in a sweet, crisp caramel, they are too good to ignore.

2 cups (12 ozs.) turbinado sugar
¼ teaspoon lemon juice
4 fl. ozs. water
1 lb. fresh figs, at room temperature

❖ Put the sugar, lemon juice and water in a small, heavy saucepan. Swirl the water around in the pan to make sure all the sugar is immersed. Heat gently, until the sugar has dissolved, swirling the pan occasionally. Continue to heat gently until the sugar solution turns a goldenbrown color.

❖ When the syrup has caramelized to a light golden brown, remove the pan from the heat. Using 2 forks, dip the figs one at a time into the syrup. Shake off the excess caramel—the coating must be thin and even—and arrange the fruit immediately on serving plates. (You will not be able to move them once the caramel sets.) Work quickly: The caramel will thicken as the figs cool it down. If this happens, reheat it gently before continuing. Serve the figs with a glass of brandy.

each serving contains:
Calories 380 • Protein 1g • Carbohydrates 100g • Fiber 1.5g

caramelized oranges with cranberries

serves 4
preparation time: 30 minutes, plus 2–3 hours chilling time
cooking time: 10–15 minutes

dried fruit (such as cranberries) is available year-round and is well worth keeping in the cupboard at all times. Throw a handful into scones, biscuits or sauces such as this one. The dried berries have a very intense flavor. Because the water has been removed, the sugar is concentrated, making the berries deliciously sweet. Make sure you remove all the bitter white pith when you peel the oranges.

½ cup (2 ozs.) dried cranberries
9 medium-size juicy oranges
1¼ cups (8 ozs.) turbinado sugar
10 fl. ozs. water
2 tablespoons Grand Marnier or brandy

❖ Put the cranberries in a bowl. Squeeze the juice from 1 orange, and pour it over the cranberries. Remove the zest from 4 oranges with a zester or vegetable peeler. Bring a small saucepan of water to a boil, add the zest, and blanch for a couple of seconds. Drain. Add the zest to the soaking cranberries. Set aside.

❖ Use a sharp serrated knife to cut the skins and pith from the remaining oranges. Carefully follow the curve of the fruit, working in small downward sections. Hold the oranges over a bowl as you work to catch any juices. Slice the oranges into rounds (discarding any seeds), and put them in a bowl.

❖ Put the sugar in a saucepan with the water. Swirl the water around in the pan to make sure all the sugar is immersed. Heat gently, until the sugar has dissolved, swirling the pan occasionally. Bring to a boil, and continue to boil until the syrup is golden. Watch carefully—if the caramel is too dark, it will taste bitter. Let cool slightly.

❖ Arrange the orange slices in a serving dish. Carefully stir any juices left in the bowl, as well as any juices left over from peeling the oranges, into the caramel. Stir in the Grand Marnier or brandy. Let the caramel cool for another 10 minutes, then pour it over the oranges. Add the cranberries, and mix carefully. Refrigerate for 2–3 hours before serving.

each serving contains:
Calories 415 • Protein 4.5g • Fat less than 1g (none saturated) • Carbohydrates 100g • Fiber 5g • Calories from fat 1% • Excellent source of vitamin C

orange custard
with cherry jam

serves 4
preparation time: 20 minutes
cooking time: 20 minutes

for a vanilla version of this custard, leave out the orange zest and juice, and add a fresh vanilla bean or vanilla extract to the milk. Soy milk contains no cholesterol and is the ideal substitute for dairy milk. Check the label on the custard powder packet to make sure it does not include animal-derived products.

for the cherry jam
½ cup (4½ ozs.) cherries, pitted
3 tablespoons turbinado sugar
a few drops of lime juice

2 tablespoons custard powder
1 tablespoon light brown sugar, softened
2 cups (1 pint) soy milk
grated zest and juice of ½ orange

❖ To make the cherry jam: Put the cherries in a saucepan, and warm gently for 5 minutes, until the juices begin to run. Crush the cherries with a potato masher, then raise the heat, and bring the juices to a boil. Stir in the sugar and lime juice, and boil rapidly for about 10 minutes, until the liquid thickens, stirring frequently. To test for a set, put a teaspoon of jam on a plate, and put the plate in the freezer for 2 minutes. Remove the plate from the freezer, and push the jam with your finger. If a crinkly skin forms on the jam, it is the right consistency. Remove the saucepan from the heat, and let cool.

❖ Combine the custard powder and sugar with about 2 tablespoons milk—just enough to form a smooth paste. Bring the remaining milk to the boiling point. Stir the paste into the hot milk, and whisk over a gentle heat, without boiling, until the custard is thick and smooth. Mix in the orange zest and juice.

❖ Divide the custard among four ramekins. Put a dollop of cherry jam in the middle of each, and serve warm or cold.

each serving contains:
Calories 150 • Protein 5g • Fat 3g (saturated 0.5g) • Carbohydrates 27g • Calories from fat 18%

plum and cinnamon crisp

serves 4
preparation time: 20 minutes
cooking time: 40 minutes

this plum crumble has a little orange zest and cinnamon mixed into the crispy topping. If you prefer, it can be made in four individual ovenproof dishes instead of one large one.

1½ lbs. fresh ripe plums, stoned and quartered
1 cup (5½ ozs.) turbinado sugar
1 cup (6 ozs.) plain flour
grated zest of ½ orange
1 teaspoon ground cinnamon
pinch of freshly grated nutmeg
pinch of salt
¼ cup (2½ ozs.) vegan margarine, chilled

❖ Preheat the oven to 375°F. Grease an ovenproof dish. Arrange the plums, cut sides up, in the dish. Combine 1 tablespoon of the sugar and 1 tablespoon of the flour, and sift them over the plums.

❖ Put the remaining sugar and flour in a bowl, and add the orange zest, cinnamon, nutmeg and salt. Cut the margarine into small pieces and, using your fingertips, rub it into the flour, until the mixture resembles bread crumbs. Sprinkle the topping over the plums.

❖ Transfer to the oven, and bake for 40 minutes, until the topping is crisp and golden brown and the plums are soft and juicy. Serve warm.

each serving contains:
Plum and cinnamon crisp: Calories 500 • Protein 5g • Fat 16g (saturated 5g) • Carbohydrates 90g • Fiber 4.5g • Calories from fat 29%
Apple and pear crisp: Calories 735 • Protein 12g • Fat 37g (saturated 6g) • Carbohydrates 93g • Fiber 8g • Calories from fat 46% • Excellent source of vitamin C
Nectarine and berry crisp: Calories 670 • Protein 8g • Fat 28g (saturated 6g) • Carbohydrates 100g • Fiber 6g • Calories from fat 39%

variations:
apple and pear crisp
Replace the plums with 1½ lbs. peeled, cored and sliced apples, and 1 cup (8 ozs.) peeled, cored and sliced pears.

nectarine and berry crisp
Replace the plums with 1½ lbs. pitted, halved and thickly sliced nectarines, and 1 lb. raspberries. Add ½ cup (1¾ ozs.) roughly chopped, toasted walnuts to the topping, and omit the cinnamon.

pancakes

serves 4
preparation time: 10 minutes, plus chilling time
cooking time: about 15 minutes

serve these pancakes in the traditional way with maple syrup, or with Fresh Fruit Compote (see page 208), Apricot Sauce (see page 217), or Apple and Brandy Sauce (see page 210).

1¼ cups (4½ ozs.) wholemeal flour
½ cup (1¾ ozs.) soy flour
8½ fl. ozs. soy milk
2 teaspoons vegetable oil, plus additional for frying
lemon juice and turbinado sugar

❖ Sieve the wholemeal and soy flours into a large mixing bowl. Gradually add the soy milk, whisking vigorously with a fork to prevent lumps from forming, to make a smooth batter. Whisk in the oil. Chill for 30 minutes.

❖ Preheat the oven to 300°F. Heat a little oil in a frying pan. As soon as it is hot, pour 2 tablespoons of the batter into the center of the pan. Swirl it around to form a thin pancake, and cook for 1 minute, until the underside is brown. Turn the pancake over, and cook the other side. Transfer to a warm serving plate, and continue until all the batter is used. Interleave the pancakes with sheets of grease-proof paper, and keep them warm in the oven. Serve with lemon juice and sugar to taste.

each serving contains:
Calories 245 • Protein 10g • Fat 13g (saturated 1.5g) •
Carbohydrates 23g • Fiber 4g • Calories from fat 47%

caramelized peach
and almond tart

serves 4–6
preparation time: 20 minutes
cooking time: 50 minutes

this tart also works well if you smooth a few tablespoons of Orange Custard (see page 200) over the base of the pastry before adding the fresh peaches. You could also replace the peaches with other fruit. Two notes: First, be sure to use pie pastry that is not derived from any animal products. Second, since this recipe calls for just 8 ounces of ready-made pie pastry, you may have a little left over.

8 ozs. ready-made pie pastry, thawed if frozen
1 lb., 5 ozs. ripe peaches
2 tablespoons confectioners' sugar
¼ cup (1 oz.) almonds
2 tablespoons apricot jam
1–2 tablespoons kirsch

❖ Preheat the oven to 375°F. Roll the pastry out to a thickness of about ¼ inch. Line a 9″ tart pan with the pastry, and prick the base all over with a fork. Chill for 30 minutes. Cover the pastry with grease-proof paper and baking beans and bake blind for 20–25 minutes, until golden and crisp.

❖ Peel the peaches, and cut them in half horizontally. Remove the stones, and slice the flesh thinly. Arrange the slices in the prebaked pastry case so that they overlap slightly. Dust the slices with the sugar. Return to the oven, and bake for 30 minutes, until the sugar is golden.

❖ Meanwhile, roughly chop the almonds. Dry-fry them in a heavy frying pan over moderate heat, turning or stirring frequently, for 5 minutes, until golden. Scatter the almonds over the cooked tart.

❖ Put the jam and kirsch in a small saucepan, and warm gently for 5 minutes, until the jam has melted. Brush the jam over the peaches, and serve the tart warm.

each serving contains:
4 servings: Calories 395 • Protein 6g • Fat 20g (saturated 6g) • Carbohydrates 51g • Fiber 4g • Calories from fat 45% • Good source of vitamin C
6 servings: Calories 265 • Protein 4g • Fat 13g (saturated 4g) • Carbohydrates 34g • Fiber 2.5g • Calories from fat 45% • Good source of vitamin C

pecan and butternut squash tart

serves 6
preparation time: 25 minutes
cooking time: 1 hour

it is always satisfying to
develop a new pastry recipe
that doesn't need butter to give
it a rich, soft, crumbly texture.
The combination of lots of nuts
with maple syrup and tahini is
delicious. I recommend using
the recipe for the base for other
tarts and pies. Or make little
tarts, and fill them with jam for
a nutty, sweet experience.

3 small butternut squash
2 fl. ozs. maple syrup
juice of 1 lemon
1 teaspoon ground cinnamon
¼ teaspoon ground cloves
1 teaspoon vanilla extract
4 fl. ozs. water
¾ cup (3 ozs.) pecans
confectioners' sugar

for the pastry
1 cup (4 ozs.) pecans
1 cup (5 ozs.) sunflower seeds
½ cup (3 ozs.) sesame seeds
2 tablespoons tahini
4 fl. ozs. maple syrup
2–4 fl. ozs. sunflower oil

❖ Preheat the oven to 350°F. Cut each butternut
squash in half lengthwise, and scoop out all the seeds
with a teaspoon. Put the squash, cut side down, on a
baking tray. Bake for 30–40 minutes, or until the flesh
is soft.
❖ Meanwhile, put all the pastry ingredients in a food
processor, and process to a thick, smooth dough.
Remove the dough from the processor, and use your
hands to flatten it to a 9″ circle. Line an 8″ pie pan
with the dough, pressing it down well. Prick all over
with a fork, and bake for 15-20 minutes, until golden
brown.

❖ Peel the butternut squash. Rinse out the bowl of the food processor. Put the flesh of the butternut squash and the maple syrup, lemon, cinnamon, cloves, vanilla extract and water in the food processor, and process until well mixed. Spoon the filling into the pastry-lined pie dish, and decorate with the pecans. Bake for 15 minutes. Let cool slightly, dust with confectioners' sugar, and cut into slices. Serve.

each serving contains:
Calories 730 • Protein 14g • Fat 55g (saturated 5g) • Carbohydrates 47g • Fiber 8g • Calories from fat 67% • Excellent source of vitamins A, B_1 (thiamin), B_3 (niacin), C and E • Good source of folic acid

treacle tart

serves 4
preparation time: 15 minutes, plus 30 minutes chilling time
cooking time: 25 minutes

treacle is also known as golden syrup, the lighter by-product of sugar refining (molasses is the darker, heavier by-product). Golden syrup can be found at better supermarkets and specialty grocers. This recipe proves that a treacle tart doesn't have to be full of butter and other dairy products to taste rich and gooey. This one is delicious served hot with a scoop of soy ice cream melting on top. Since this recipe calls for just 6½ ounces of ready-made pie pastry, you may have a little left over.

6½ ozs. ready-made pie pastry, thawed if frozen
1 cup (8 ozs.) golden syrup
finely grated zest and juice of 1 lemon
1 cup (2½ ozs.) fresh white bread crumbs

❖ Roll the pastry out on a lightly floured surface to a thickness of about ¼ inch. Line an 8″ tart pan with the pastry, and prick the base all over with a fork. Chill for 30 minutes.

❖ Meanwhile, preheat the oven to 375°F. Warm the syrup gently in a saucepan, then add the lemon zest and juice. Scatter the bread crumbs over the pastry base, and slowly pour in the syrup. Bake in the oven for 25 minutes, until the filling is just set. Serve warm.

each serving contains:
Calories 430 • Protein 5g • Fat 12g (saturated 4g) • Carbohydrates 79g • Fiber 1g • Calories from fat 26%

baked bananas
with orange and hazelnuts

serves 4
preparation time: 15 minutes
cooking time: 20 minutes

this is a hot version of a banana sundae. As with all nuts, dry-frying the hazelnuts really brings out their flavor.

4 firm bananas, unpeeled
1 tablespoon lemon juice
1¼ cups (4½ ozs.) hazelnuts, roughly chopped
4 scoops soy ice cream
juice of ½ orange

❖ Preheat the oven to 400°F. Put the bananas on a baking tray, and brush them with the lemon juice. Bake for 20 minutes, or until they are dark and soft.
❖ Meanwhile, dry-fry the hazelnuts in a heavy frying pan over moderate heat, turning or stirring frequently, for 5 minutes, until golden. Roughly chop the nuts.
❖ Snip open the banana skins with scissors or a knife, and put a scoop of ice cream in the middle of each one. Drizzle the orange juice over the ice cream, and scatter the hazelnuts on top. Serve immediately.

each serving contains:
Calories 400 • Protein 7.5g • Fat 25g (saturated 4g) •
Carbohydrates 39g • Fiber 3g • Calories from fat 56%

banana flapjacks with fresh fruit compote

makes 12 flapjacks
preparation time: 20 minutes
cooking time: 25–30 minutes

the protein in Brazil nuts is high in methionine, the amino acid that is often in shortest supply in a vegan diet. More important, these flapjacks look as tempting as they taste. Serve them on individual plates, as I suggest, or pile them up on a large dish, and accompany with a bowl of the compote.

for the compote

1 lb. fresh strawberries, hulled
1/2 cup (4 ozs.) blueberries
1/2 cup (4 ozs.) blackberries
1/2 cup (4 ozs.) raspberries
4 teaspoons sugar
1/2 teaspoon kirsch

1/2 cup (1 3/4 ozs.) Brazil nuts, roughly chopped
1/2 cup (4 ozs.) margarine
1/2 cup (2 1/2 ozs.) light brown sugar, softened
2 tablespoons corn syrup
5 1/4 cups (13 ozs.) old-fashioned rolled oats
1/2 teaspoon baking powder
2 ripe bananas, mashed

❖ Preheat the oven to 350°F. To make the compote: Combine the strawberries, blueberries, blackberries and raspberries in a bowl. Sprinkle in the sugar and kirsch, and mix well. Chill until needed.

❖ Dry-fry the Brazil nuts in a heavy frying pan over moderate heat, turning or stirring frequently, for 5 minutes, until golden.

❖ Lightly grease a 9″ × 13″ Swiss roll pan. Put the margarine, sugar and corn syrup in a large saucepan, and stir over low heat for 5 minutes, until melted. Mix in the Brazil nuts, rolled oats and baking powder. Add the bananas, and mix well. Spread the mixture out on the Swiss roll pan, and bake for 20 minutes, or until the edges are beginning to turn golden. Cut into squares while still warm. Let cool slightly on the pan, then transfer to a wire rack to finish cooling.

❖ Divide the flapjacks among four plates. Add a spoonful of compote to each portion, and serve.

each serving contains:
Calories 620 • Protein 10g • Fat 27g (saturated 6g) • Carbohydrates 88g • Fiber 7g • Calories from fat 39% • Excellent source of vitamin C • Good source of vitamins B_1 (thiamin) and E

walnut layer with apple and brandy sauce

serves 4
preparation time: 20–25 minutes
cooking time: 15–17 minutes

handle the walnut dough lightly so that it is crisp and light when cooked. The more you handle it, the harder and tougher it will become.

¾ cup (3½ ozs.) walnuts
½ cup (4 ozs.) margarine
½ cup (2 ozs.) light brown sugar, softened
1 cup (4 ozs.) self-rising flour
4 tablespoons turbinado sugar
confectioners' sugar

for the apple and brandy sauce
2½ lbs. apples
juice of 1 lemon
2 tablespoons calvados
1 tablespoon sugar
2 tablespoons apple jelly

❖ Preheat the oven to 350°F. Preheat the grill to high. Spread the walnuts on a baking tray, and toast them under the grill for 5 minutes, or until golden. Let cool, then chop finely.

❖ Lightly grease a baking sheet. Put the margarine and brown sugar in a bowl, and beat well with a wooden spoon, until light and fluffy. Add half the walnuts and the flour and, using your hands, work them together to form a dough that comes away from the sides of the bowl. Gently knead the dough until smooth. Transfer the dough to a floured surface, and lightly roll it out to form a rectangle about ¼″ thick. Use an upturned plate to cut 2 circles about 6 inches in diameter. Place the pastry circles on the baking sheet, and bake for 10–12 minutes, until pale golden. Use the point of a knife to lightly mark each circle into quarters. Sprinkle the turbinado sugar over the circles, and let cool until crisp.

❖ To make the apple and brandy sauce: Peel the apples, and cut into small chunks. Toss in the lemon juice. Put the apples and calvados in a saucepan. Cover, bring to a simmer, and simmer for 15 minutes. Add the sugar and apple jelly. Simmer, stirring, for 5 minutes, or until the apples form a thick puree.

❖ Slice each pastry circle into quarters along the marked lines. Put 1 quarter on a plate, spread 2 tablespoons apple and brandy sauce over it, and cover with another quarter. Spoon a little sauce over the top. Sprinkle with a few of the remaining walnuts, and dust with confectioners' sugar. Repeat with the remaining pastry quarters and sauce. Serve.

each serving contains:
Calories 785 • Protein 7g • Fat 41g (saturated 8g) • Carbohydrates 100g • Fiber 6g • Calories from fat 47% • Good source of vitamins A and C

sponge cake with strawberries and lemon balm

serves 6–8
preparation time: 20 minutes
cooking time: 25–30 minutes

this cake is both light and rich—and perfect when it's filled with fresh berries and a little sweet jam. I have used lemon balm leaves, but fresh mint leaves are just as good. (You may be able to find lemon balm leaves in health food stores.) I never like to give quantities of sugar to add to fruit. Its sweetness level varies so much that it is best to sweeten fruit to taste.

½ cup (4½ ozs.) margarine
½ cup (2½ ozs.) turbinado sugar
2¼ cups (9 ozs.) self-rising flour
3 teaspoons baking powder
pinch of sea salt
9 fl. ozs. soy yogurt
¼ teaspoon vanilla extract
1–2 tablespoons soy milk

for the filling
1 lb. strawberries, sliced
sugar and orange liqueur, to taste
4 tablespoons strawberry jam

to decorate
confectioners' sugar
handful of lemon balm or fresh mint leaves

❖ Preheat the oven to 350°F. Put the margarine and sugar in a saucepan, and heat gently, until the sugar has dissolved. Let cool.

❖ Grease an 8″ cake pan, and line the base with grease-proof paper. Sieve the flour and baking powder into a bowl, and add the salt. Pour the margarine and sugar into the dry ingredients, and add the yogurt and vanilla extract. Mix well with a wooden spoon, until the mixture reaches a soft dropping consistency. Add a little soy milk if necessary. Spoon the cake mixture into the pan, and bake for 20–25 minutes, until risen and golden. The center should feel springy if you touch it with your fingertips. Let cool.

❖ Cut the cake in half horizontally. Put the strawberries in a bowl, and add sugar and orange liqueur to taste. Spread a layer of jam over the tops of both halves of the cake. Cover one half with a layer of half the sliced strawberries, and put the other half, jam side up, on top of it. Arrange the remaining berries on the jam, and dust with confectioners' sugar. Scatter a few fresh lemon balm or mint leaves over the top, and serve.

each serving contains:
6 servings: Calories 480 • Protein 6.5g • Fat 19g (saturated 8g) • Carbohydrates 73g • Fiber 2g • Calories from fat 37% • Excellent source of vitamin C • Good source of vitamin A
8 servings: Calories 360 • Protein 5g • Fat 14.5g (saturated 6g) • Carbohydrates 55g • Fiber 1.5g • Calories from fat 37% • Excellent source of vitamin C • Good source of vitamin A

chocolate raspberry hazelnut cake

serves 10
preparation time: 20 minutes
cooking time: 45 minutes

this is a chocolate cake for vegans that tastes as good as any I've ever tasted. I decided that I would not include a chocolate cake unless it was really chocolately, absolutely delicious and, most important, gooey in the middle, as all good chocolate cakes are. This one is all of these and more. It can be served hot with crushed raspberries as a dessert, or cold with a cup of tea in the middle of the afternoon. It is important to use frozen, not fresh, raspberries; they keep their shape much better.

½ cup (2 ozs.) hazelnuts
2¼ cups (9 ozs.) self-rising flour
¾ cup (3 ozs.) cocoa powder
3 teaspoons baking powder
1½ cups (9 ozs.) turbinado sugar
1½ teaspoons vanilla extract (optional)
4 fl. ozs. corn oil
12 fl. ozs. soy milk
½ cup (4½ ozs.) frozen raspberries
confectioners' sugar

❖ Preheat the oven to 350°F. Preheat the grill to high. Spread the hazelnuts on a baking tray. Toast them on the grill, turning frequently, for 5 minutes, or until golden. Cool, then chop finely. Grease an 8″ cake pan, and line the base with greaseproof paper.

❖ Sift the flour, cocoa powder and baking powder into a bowl. Mix in the sugar, then add the vanilla extract, if using, oil and soy milk. Beat the mixture with an electric mixer, until it has the consistency of a thick batter. Stir in the raspberries and hazelnuts. Pour into the pan, and bake for 40 minutes, until the outside of the cake is cooked and the center is still slightly squishy. Cool on a wire rack. Alternatively, serve the cake warm as a dessert. Either way, dust the top with confectioners' sugar before serving.

each serving contains:
Calories 335 • Protein 6g • Fat 15g (saturated 3g) • Carbohydrates 47g • Fiber 2.5g • Calories from fat 40% • Good source of vitamin E

apricot and raspberry cobbler

serves 4
preparation time: 20 minutes
cooking time: 35–45 minutes

this is comforting and delicious cobbler. You can substitute seasonal fruit for the apricots and raspberries. Pears and blackberries work well, as do apples and blueberries. Serve with soy yogurt.

1½ lbs. fresh apricots, pitted and halved
1 cup (8 ozs.) raspberries
2 tablespoons (1 oz.) sugar
1 cup (3½ ozs.) self-rising flour
2 tablespoons (½ oz.) ground almonds
¼ teaspoon baking powder
pinch of salt
½ teaspoon cinnamon
pinch of grated fresh nutmeg
1½ tablespoons turbinado sugar, plus extra for dusting
1 teaspoon vanilla extract
2 tablespoons corn oil
4 tablespoons soy milk

❖ Preheat the oven to 400°F. Put the apricots, raspberries, sugar and water in a saucepan, and cook gently for about 3 minutes, until soft. Pour into an ovenproof serving dish. Set aside.

❖ Sift the flour, almonds, baking powder, salt, cinnamon and nutmeg into a bowl. Stir in the sugar. Make a well in the middle of the dry ingredients. Mix the vanilla, corn oil and milk, and pour the liquid into the well. Mix well, drawing the dry ingredients into the liquid with a wooden spoon. Do not beat. The mixture should take on a dropping consistency. Drop 10 small spoonfuls of the mixture on top of the fruit, and dust with a little sugar. Bake for 30–40 minutes, until the topping is risen and golden. Serve warm.

each serving contains:
Calories 275 • Protein 6g • Fat 8.5g (saturated 1g) • Carbohydrates 46g • Fiber 5g • Calories from fat 28% • Good source of vitamin C

crispy cinnamon bread knots with apricot sauce

serves 6–8
preparation time: 20 minutes, plus 2 hours rising time
cooking time: 30 minutes, cooked in batches

this is a pudding that everyone loves, especially children. Make the bread knots when you have something to do during the couple of hours the dough will take to rise. Aside from the rising time, it won't take long to prepare and cook them.

2½ cups (10 ozs.) plain flour
2 teaspoons ground cinnamon, plus extra for dusting
½ teaspoon freshly grated nutmeg
¾ cup turbinado sugar
pinch of salt
1 packet (¼-oz.) Rapid Rise yeast
1 teaspoon vanilla extract
5-7 tablespoons fl. ozs. tepid water
corn oil, for deep-frying
confectioners' sugar, for dusting

for the apricot sauce
7 tablespoons (3½ ozs.) turbinado sugar
juice of 2 oranges
4 tablespoons water
1 lb. dried apricots
2 tablespoons amaretto liqueur

❖ Sift the flour, cinnamon, nutmeg, sugar and salt into a bowl. Make a well in the middle, and stir in the yeast and vanilla extract. Gradually pour in the water—enough to make a soft dough. As you pour the water in, use a wooden spoon to bring the flour into it from around the edges. You may find it easier to use your hands toward the end of the process. Transfer the dough to a floured surface, and knead it with your fingers and the palm of your hand for about 10–15 minutes, until it is soft and elastic. Put the dough in a covered bowl, and let it rise in a warm place for about 2 hours, until it is 3 to 4 times its original size.

❖ Meanwhile, make the apricot sauce: Put the sugar and orange juice in a saucepan with 4 tablespoons water and heat gently until the sugar has dissolved. Add the apricots, cover and simmer for 10–15 minutes, until the fruit is plump and soft. Pour the contents of the saucepan into a food processor, add the liqueur, and process to a coarse puree. Stir in enough water to make a smooth sauce. Pour the sauce into a saucepan. Warm the sauce gently when you are ready to serve the bread knots.

❖ When the dough has risen, half-fill a deep fryer or a deep, heavy saucepan with the corn oil, and heat to 375°F. To test the temperature, drop a cube of bread in the oil—it should brown within 1 minute. Knead the dough again until it is smooth and even. Grease your hands with a little oil, and pinch off small pieces of dough. Roll the pieces into 5- to 6-inch lengths, and tie each length into a knot. Drop 2 or 3 knots into the hot oil. Fry them, turning them frequently, for 2–4 minutes, until golden brown and puffy. Drain on paper towels. Repeat with the remaining knots. Dust with confectioners' sugar and cinnamon, and serve immediately with the warm apricot sauce as an accompaniment.

each serving contains:
6 servings: Calories 514 • Protein 8g • Fat 14g (saturated 1g) • Carbohydrates 93g • Fiber 7g • Calories from fat 24%
8 servings: Calories 385 • Protein 6g • Fat 10g (saturated 1g) • Carbohydrates 74g • Fiber 5g • Calories from fat 24%

winter fruit salad

serves 4
preparation time: 20 minutes
cooking time: 1 hour

imagine hot fruit soaked in a rich sauce made of brandy, orange juice and ginger syrup and served in wine glasses. A cinnamon stick popped into each glass and a sprinkling of ground cinnamon provide the kind of finishing touch that transforms a traditional dish into something modern and fresh.

¼ cup (2 ozs.) dried prunes, pitted
2 York Imperial apples, peeled, cored and thinly sliced
¼ cup (2 ozs.) dried figs
½ cup (2 ozs.) dried apricots
1 small pineapple, peeled, cored and diced
2 tablespoons calvados or brandy of your choice
juice and zest of 1 orange
1 tablespoon ginger syrup from the preserved candied ginger (see below)
3 tablespoons (1 oz.) turbinado sugar

to decorate
large handful of cashews
large handful of hazelnuts
1 piece of sweet red candied ginger, packed in red ginger syrup, drained and cut into fine strips
4 cinnamon sticks
large pinch of ground cinnamon

❖ Preheat the oven to 350°F. Put the prunes, apples, figs, apricots, pineapple, calvados or brandy, orange zest and juice, ginger syrup and sugar in an ovenproof dish. Mix well. Cover with a lid or aluminium foil, and bake for 1 hour.

❖ Meanwhile, preheat the grill to high. Spread the cashews and hazelnuts on a baking tray. Toast them on the grill, turning frequently, for 5 minutes, or until golden. Cool, then chop roughly.

❖ Divide the hot fruit among four wine glasses. Scatter the toasted cashews and hazelnuts and the candied ginger strips over the top. Pop a cinnamon stick into each glass, sprinkle with ground cinnamon, and serve.

each serving contains:
Calories 235 • Protein 3g • Fat 5g
(saturated 0.5g) • Carbohydrates 43g •
Fiber 5g • Calories from fat 18% • Good
source of vitamin C

menus

when you are planning a menu, the nutritional balance of each course is just the start. Flavors, colors and textures of the food all need to be considered. The courses must be both complementary and contrasting. You will also have to consider the time available for preparation and cooking, and the kind of meal you want to serve.

a supper party

Choose dishes that can be doubled or tripled to accommodate the number of guests. The menu needs to be relaxed and casual, but still impressive. The preparation should be done before your guests arrive.

Make a selection of "nibbles" that you can put in bowls around the room so that people can eat when they choose:

❖ cayenne chips, hot and spicy popcorn, coriander spiced nuts

Serve the Cayenne Chips first. If you serve hot and cold nibbles at the same time, guests may leave the hot food until it has gone cold.

❖ juma's african curry tuscan tarts
❖ chocolate raspberry hazelnut cake
   (serve with a big bowl of crushed raspberries)
❖ treacle tart

a supper to prepare ahead

This is a menu for those occasions when you have friends staying with you and you want to take them out for the day, but also want to serve them a delicious supper in the evening. Prepare these dishes the day before, and simply heat and assemble them when you are ready to eat.

❖ melon with toasted seeds
❖ pacific rim coconut curry
❖ moroccan spiced rice pudding

sunday lunch

The emphasis here is food for the whole family. You want everyone to be relaxed and happy and to enjoy the day. Time is not as important as it often is during the week, so you can serve a meal that may take a while to cook or prepare—but get everyone into the kitchen to help.

❖ roasted apple, onion and potato soup
   (serve with parsley and garlic pita toasts)
❖ vegan lasagna (serve with a fresh green salad)
❖ pecan and butternut squash tart or coconut ice dessert with chocolate sauce

romantic meal for two

Food is sensual. For this light, but very satisfying, menu, I have chosen food that you can eat with your hands or feed to each other.

- ❖ baked asparagus with garlic croutons
- ❖ vegan sushi with pickled ginger and soy sauce
- ❖ orange and passionfruit sorbet or fresh fruit in wine with fresh basil

a dinner for his/her parents

Planning and preparation are the key to a successful dinner party—even more so when you want to really impress your guests. Choose dishes that can be made in advance, allowing you to relax and entertain your guests without having to worry about the food.

- ❖ creamy carrot and ginger soup (serve with crispy curls of toast)
- ❖ moroccan-style chickpeas with saffron rice
- ❖ plum and cinnamon crisp

a quick lunch

There are always occasions when we want to invite friends for lunch on Saturday, but don't want to spend hours preparing the food. This menu is perfect for those situations. The flap-jacks can be made in advance and frozen until needed. If you are lucky enough to have good weather, food such as this can be enjoyed in the garden.

- ❖ pureed chickpeas with stir-fried vegetables
- ❖ bright red pepper linguine
- ❖ banana flapjacks with fresh fruit compote

a picnic

All the following recipes are quick to prepare and easy to transport: take the gazpacho in an insulated container and put the croutons, and the salad or sandwiches in separate picnic boxes or containers. Don't forget the pepper mill for the strawberries and black pepper.

- ❖ spicy gazpacho soup with paprika croutons
- ❖ summer pasta salad or thai vegetables in fresh herb bread
- ❖ strawberries with black pepper

a special event

A wonderful dish of wild mushrooms with crushed red peppercorns and garlic is a fabulous way to start a celebratory meal. The lemon sherbet will clear the palate before you serve the impressive tarts.

❖ mushrooms with peppercorns and garlic
❖ lemon sherbet cups (without the crushed blueberries)
❖ sticky golden onion tarts
❖ fruit with cardamom and vanilla

index

❖ a

Almond Tart, Caramelized Peach and, 203
Apples
    Apple and Pear Crisp, 201
    Roasted Apple, Onion and Sweet Potato Soup,
        50–51
    Walnut Layer with Apple and Brandy Sauce,
        210–11
Apricots
    Apricot and Raspberry Cobbler, 215
    Apricot Sauce, 216–17
    Fresh Fruit in Wine with Basil, 196
    Poached Fruit in Lavender-Infused Syrup with
        Toffee Crisps, 186
Asparagus with Garlic Croutons, Baked, 38
Avocados
    Avocado Butter with Tomato Relish in Focaccia,
        106
    Avocado with Beans and Cilantro, 49
    Pureed Avocado Dip with Pickled Ginger and
        Wasabi, 23
    Salad of Ciabatta Croutons with Avocado,
        Grapefruit and Vinaigrette, 97
    Vegan Sushi with Avocado and Cucumber, 120–21

❖ b

B vitamins, 6
Baby Mediterranean Tarts with Fresh Basil Puree, 45
Baked Asparagus with Garlic Croutons, 38
Baked Bananas with Oranges and Hazelnuts, 207

Baked Pears and Ginger, 184
Balsamic White Peach Salad with Parsley Shortcakes,
    88–89
Balti, 154–55
Bananas
    Baked Bananas with Oranges and Hazelnuts, 207
    Banana Flapjacks with Fresh Fruit Compote,
        208–9
    Fresh Fruit in Wine with Basil, 196
    Fruit with Cardamom and Vanilla, 187
Basmati and Wild Rice Salad, 99
Beans
    See also Chickpeas
    Avocado with Beans and Cilantro, 49
    Fresh Broad Beans with Paprika and Lemon, 81
    Polenta with Beans, 138
    Potatoes with Broad Beans and Mint Vinaigrette,
        48
    Puree of Beans and Potatoes with Olive Oil, 75
    Stir-Fried Black Beans with Lime and Chili,
        156–57
    Warm Butter Bean Puree, 36–37
    Warm Lemon and Olive Oil Beans on Rosemary
        Mashed Potatoes, 84–85
Beets
    Vegetable Chips, 25
    with Vinaigrette, 39
    Vivid Beet with Horseradish Gnocchi, 74
Berries, 15
    Nectarine and Berry Crisp, 201

Black Beans with Lime and Chili, Stir-Fried, 156–57
Blood Oranges with Red Onions, Black Olives, and
    Fennel Dressing, 47
Blueberries
    Fruit with Cardamom and Vanilla, 187
    Lemon Sherbet Cups with Crushed Blueberries,
    194
Bok Choy with Soy Sauce and Toasted Seeds, Steamed,
    29
Bread
    Avocado Butter with Tomato Relish in Focaccia,
    106
    Crispy Cinnamon Bread Knots with Apricot Sauce,
    216–17
    Four-Onion Croustades, 80
    Fried Tomato Toasts, 46
    frozen, 15
    Parsley and Garlic Pita Toasts, 34
    Pita Bread with Garlic Cream and Fresh Lime, 104
    Spicy Satay on White Bread, 98
    Thai Vegetables in Fresh Herb Bread, 105
Bright Red Pepper Pesto Linguine, 68
Broad beans, 15
    Fresh Broad Beans with Paprika and Lemon, 81
    Potatoes with Broad Beans and Mint Vinaigrette, 48
Butter Bean Puree, Warm, 36–37
Butternut Squash
    Pecan and Butternut Squash Tart, 204–5
    Roasted Squash Soup with Fresh Cilantro, 59

❖ C
Cabbage
    Red Cabbage Relish with Parsley Mashed Potatoes,
    90
    Red Cabbage with Sake on Rice Noodles,
    122
Cakes
    Chocolate Raspberry Hazelnut Cake, 214
    Sponge Cake with Strawberries and Lemon Balm,
    212–13
Calcium, 7
Caramelized Fennel and Shallot Risotto, 124
Caramelized Oranges with Cranberries, 199
Caramelized Peach and Almond Tart, 203
Carbohydrates, 7
Carrots
    Creamy Carrot and Ginger Soup with Curly Toasts,
    53
    with Mint and Lime Dressing in Pita Bread, 107
    Spicy Vegetable Rounds with Chunky Tomato
    Chutney, 170–71
Cayenne Chips, 26
Cherry Jam, Orange Custard with, 200
Chickpeas
    Balti, 154–55
    Moroccan Spiced Couscous with Fruit, 64–65
    Moroccan Spiced Red Potato with Chickpeas,
    148–49
    Moroccan-Style Chickpeas with Saffron Rice,
    172–73
    Pureed Chickpeas with Stir-Fried Vegetables, 35
    Vegetables in a Crispy Chickpea Batter, 32–33

Chili and Cilantro Corn Fritters with Tomato Sauce,
    92–93
Chili Pakoras with Chunky Tomato Chutney, 30–31
Chilied Spring Rolls with Dipping Sauce, 136–37
Chilies, 13
Chips
    Cayenne, 26
    Vegetable, 25
Chocolate
    Chocolate Raspberry Hazelnut Cake, 214
    Coconut Ice Dessert with Chocolate Sauce,
    192–93
Chutneys
    Chunky Tomato Chutney, 170–71
    Cilantro Chutney, 142–43
    Peach and Lemon Grass Chutney, 146–47
    Samosas with Mango Chutney, 76–77
Cilantro
    Avocado with Beans and Cilantro, 49
    Chili and Cilantro Corn Fritters with Tomato
    Sauce, 92–93
    Chutney, 142–43
    Eggplant Slices with Lemon and Cilantro, 162
    New Potatoes and Small Peas with Pungent Green
    Sauce, 163
    Papaya and Cilantro Salsa on Coconut Rice, 91
    Roasted Squash Soup with Fresh Cilantro, 59
    Tomato Soup with Cilantro Salsa, 54
Coconut
    Coconut Ice Dessert with Chocolate Sauce,
    192–93
    Coconut Rice Pudding with Mango and Papaya,
    181
    Corn, Coconut, Lime and Basil Soup, 56–57
    Malaysian Vegetables, 141
    milk, 10
    Pacific Rim Coconut Curry, 164–65
    Papaya and Coconut Sherbet, 190–91
    Spicy Vegetables and Coconut Cream, 130–31
    Thai Pumpkin and Coconut Soup, 52
Coriander Spiced Nuts, 19
Corn
    Chili and Cilantro Corn Fritters with Tomato
    Sauce, 92–93
    Corn, Coconut, Lime and Basil Soup, 56–57
    Hot and Spicy Popcorn, 20
Couscous
    Griddled Red Onion Slices with Couscous, 66
    Moroccan Spiced Couscous with Fruit, 64–65
    Roasted Vegetables with Couscous and Lemon
    Pepper Oil, 144–45
    Warm Couscous with Garlic, Black Olives and
    Tomatoes, 67
Cranberries, Caramelized Oranges with, 199
Creamy Carrot and Ginger Soup with Curly Toasts, 53
Crispy Cinnamon Bread Knots with Apricot Sauce,
    216–17
Crispy Polenta Peppers and Zucchini with Balsamic
    Vinegar, 166
Croustades, Four-Onion, 80
Croutons
    Ciabatta, 97

garlic, 38
paprika, 60
Crunchy Baked Tomatoes with Lime, Onion, and Chili, 44
Curries
    Juma's Special African Curry, 132–33
    Pacific Rim Coconut Curry, 164–65
    Thai Green Vegetable Curry, 158–59
Custard with Cherry Jam, Orange, 200

❖ d

Desserts, 180–218
    Apple and Pear Crisp, 201
    Apricot and Raspberry Cobbler, 215
    Baked Bananas with Oranges and Hazelnuts, 207
    Baked Pears and Ginger, 184
    Banana Flapjacks with Fresh Fruit Compote, 208–9
    Caramelized Oranges with Cranberries, 199
    Caramelized Peach and Almond Tart, 203
    Chocolate Raspberry Hazelnut Cake, 214
    Coconut Ice Dessert with Chocolate Sauce, 192–93
    Coconut Rice Pudding with Mango and Papaya, 181
    Crispy Cinnamon Bread Knots with Apricot Sauce, 216–17
    Fresh Fruit in Wine with Basil, 196
    Frozen Yogurt Crunch with Raspberry Sauce, 195
    Fruit with Cardamom and Vanilla, 187
    Hot Poached Pears with Toffee Crisps, 185
    Lemon Sherbet Cups with Crushed Blueberries, 194
    Moroccan Spiced Rice Pudding, 182–83
    Nectarine and Berry Crisp, 201
    Orange and Passion Fruit Sorbet, 188–89
    Orange Custard with Cherry Jam, 200
    Pancakes, 202
    Papaya and Coconut Sherbet, 190–91
    Pecan and Butternut Squash Tart, 204–5
    Plum and Cinnamon Crisp, 201
    Poached Fruit in Lavender-Infused Syrup with Toffee Crisps, 186
    Sponge Cake with Strawberries and Lemon Balm, 212–13
    Strawberries with Black Pepper, 197
    Toffee Figs with a Glass of Brandy, 198
    Treacle Tart, 206
    Walnut Layer with Apple and Brandy Sauce, 210–11
    Warm Hazelnut Scones with Fruit Salsa, 180
    Winter Fruit Salad, 218
Dips
    Avocado Butter, 106
    Lemon Tahini, 24
    Pureed Avocado Dip with Pickled Ginger and Wasabi, 23
    Warm Butter Bean Puree, 36–37
Dressings
    Black Olive, 91
    Chili and Lemon Grass Dressing, 118–19
    Fennel Dressing, 47
    Garlicky Vinaigrette, 100
    Mint and Lime, 107
    Mint Vinaigrette, 48
    Vinaigrette, 97
Dried fruit, 10

❖ e

Eggplant
    Butter with Sea Salt-Crusted Potatoes, 160–61
    Grilled Eggplant with Black Olive Dressing, 94
    Pacific Rim Coconut Curry, 164–65
    and Potato Bake, 151
    Slices with Lemon and Cilantro, 162
    Warm Tomato and Eggplant Stacks, 82–83

❖ f

Fat, 7
Fennel
    Blood Oranges with Red Onions, Black Olives, and Fennel Dressing, 47
    Caramelized Fennel and Shallot Risotto, 124
    and Ginger Tarts, 79
Figs with a Glass of Brandy, Toffee, 198
Four-Onion Croustades, 80
Freezer, stocking the, 14–15
Fresh Broad Beans with Paprika and Lemon, 81
Fresh Fruit in Wine with Basil, 196
Fresh Ginger and Basil Pasta, 69
Fridge, stocking the, 13–14
Fried Tomato Toasts, 46
Frozen Yogurt Crunch with Raspberry Sauce, 195
Fruit
    See also Apples, Raspberries, etc.
    Banana Flapjacks with Fresh Fruit Compote, 208–9
    with Cardamom and Vanilla, 187
    dried, 10
    Fresh Fruit in Wine with Basil, 196
    Moroccan Spiced Couscous with Fruit, 64–65
    Poached Fruit in Lavender-Infused Syrup with Toffee Crisps, 186
    Salsa, 180
    Winter Fruit Salad, 218

❖ g

Garbanzos. See Chickpeas
Garlic Croutons, 38
Gazpacho Soup with Paprika Croutons, Spicy, 60–61
Ginger, 13
    Baked Pears and Ginger, 184
    Creamy Carrot and Ginger Soup with Curly Toasts, 53
    Fennel and Ginger Tarts, 79
    Fresh Ginger and Basil Pasta, 69
    pickled, 16
    Pureed Avocado Dip with Pickled Ginger and Wasabi, 23
Gnocchi
    with Tomatoes and Fresh Mint, 113
    Vivid Beet with Horseradish Gnocchi, 74
Grains, 10
    See also Couscous; Rice
Grapefruit, Salad of Ciabatta Croutons with Avocado, and Vinaigrette, 97

Grapes, 185
Griddled Red Onion Slices with Couscous, 66
Grilled Eggplant with Black Olive Dressing, 94
Grilled Vegetables on Lemon Grass Sticks with
    Coriander Basmati, 142–43

❖ h
Hazelnuts
    Baked Bananas with Oranges and Hazelnuts, 207
    Chocolate Raspberry Hazelnut Cake, 214
    Warm Hazelnut Scones with Fruit Salsa, 180
Health, vegan diet and, 5–6
Herbs, 14
Homemade Pizzas, 176–77
Honey, 16
Hot and Spicy Popcorn, 20
Hot Grilled Sweet Potato with Watercress Salsa, 40–41
Hot Poached Pears with Toffee Crisps, 185

❖ i
Ice cream, 15
Indian Vegetables, 152–53
Individual Crispy Porcini Bakes, 168–69
Ingredients, 2–3, 8, 9–16
Iron, 7

❖ j
Jams, 10
    Cherry Jam, 200
Japanese Rice Bowl with Vegetables, 126–27
Juma's Special African Curry, 132–33

❖ k
Kaffir lime leaves, 16

❖ l
Lasagna, Vegan, 174–75
Legumes, 11
    See also Beans
Lemon grass, 14
    Grilled Vegetables on Lemon Grass Sticks with
        Coriander Basmati, 142–43
    Peach and Lemon Grass Chutney, 146–47
    Thai Noodles with Chili and Lemon Grass
        Dressing, 118–19
Lemons, 14
    Fresh Broad Beans with Paprika and Lemon, 81
    Lemon Sherbet Cups with Crushed Blueberries,
        194
    Lemon Tahini Dip, 24
    Sponge Cake with Strawberries and Lemon Balm,
        212–13
    Warm Lemon and Olive Oil Beans on Rosemary
        Mashed Potatoes, 84–85
Limes, 14
    Corn, Coconut, Lime and Basil Soup, 56–57
    Crunchy Baked Tomatoes with Lime, Onion, and
        Chili, 44
    Pita Bread with Garlic Cream and Fresh Lime, 104

❖ m
Main courses, 110–77

Balti, 154–55
Caramelized Fennel and Shallot Risotto, 124
Chilied Spring Rolls with Dipping Sauce, 136–37
Crispy Polenta Peppers and Zucchini with Balsamic
    Vinegar, 166
Eggplant and Potato Bake, 151
Eggplant Butter with Sea Salt-Crusted Potatoes,
    160–61
Eggplant Slices with Lemon and Cilantro, 162
Gnocchi with Tomatoes and Fresh Mint, 113
Grilled Vegetables on Lemon Grass Sticks with
    Coriander Basmati, 142–43
Homemade Pizzas, 176–77
Indian Vegetables, 152–53
Individual Crispy Porcini Bakes, 168–69
Japanese Rice Bowl with Vegetables, 126–27
Juma's Special African Curry, 132–33
Malaysian Vegetables, 141
Mediterranean Potatoes with Olives, Herbs and
    Tomatoes, 150
Mixed Mushrooms and Tofu Pasta, 114–15
Moroccan Pilaf, 125
Moroccan Spiced Red Potato with Chickpeas,
    148–49
Moroccan-Style Chickpeas with Saffron Rice,
    172–73
New Potatoes and Small Peas with Pungent Green
    Sauce, 163
Pacific Rim Coconut Curry, 164–65
Polenta with Beans, 138
Potato Cakes with Peach and Lemon Grass
    Chutney, 146–47
Red Cabbage with Sake on Rice Noodles, 122
Roasted Garlic and Walnut Linguine, 117
Roasted Garlic Polenta with Sautéed Tomatoes,
    110–11
Roasted Red Onions and Wilted Spinach with
    Sweet Potatoes, 167
Roasted Vegetables with Couscous and Lemon
    Pepper Oil, 144–45
Spaghetti with Tomato Sauce, 116
Spicy Vegetable Rounds with Chunky Tomato
    Chutney, 170–71
Spicy Vegetables and Coconut Cream, 130–31
Spring Vegetables with Saffron Basmati Rice,
    128–29
Sticky Golden Onion Tarts, 139
Stir-Fried Black Beans with Lime and Chili, 156–57
Thai Green Vegetable Curry, 158–59
Thai Noodles with Chili and Lemon Grass
    Dressing, 118–19
Tomato and Basil Risotto, 123
Tomato and Pine Nut Linguine with Caramelized
    Lemon, 112
Tuscan Tarts, 140
Vegan Lasagna, 174–75
Vegan Sushi with Avocado and Cucumber, 120–21
Wontons with Chili Sauce, 134–35
Malaysian Vegetables, 141
Mango
    Coconut Rice Pudding with Mango and Papaya, 181
    Fresh Fruit in Wine with Basil, 196

Samosas with Mango Chutney, 76–77
Margarine, vegan, 14
Mediterranean Galette, 78
Mediterranean Potatoes with Olives, Herbs and
    Tomatoes, 150
Melon
    with Red Wine and Mint Sauce, 27
    with Toasted Seeds, 28
Menus, 219–22
Minerals, 6
Mint Vinaigrette, 48
Mixed Mushrooms and Tofu Pasta, 114–15
Modern Waldorf Salad, 101
Moroccan Pilaf, 125
Moroccan Spiced Couscous with Fruit, 64–65
Moroccan Spiced Red Potato with Chickpeas, 148–49
Moroccan Spiced Rice Pudding, 182–83
Moroccan-Style Chickpeas with Saffron Rice, 172–73
Mushrooms
    Individual Crispy Porcini Bakes, 168–69
    Mediterranean Galette, 78
    Mixed Mushrooms and Tofu Pasta, 114–15
    Mushrooms with Peppercorns and Garlic, 43
    Rich Mushroom Sauce with Tagliatelle, 73
    Rich Mushrooms on Toast with Truffle Oil, 42
    Vegan Lasagna, 174–75
    Wild Mushroom Soup, 58
    Wontons with Chili Sauce, 134–35

❖ n
Nectarine and Berry Crisp, 201
New Potatoes and Small Peas with Pungent Green
    Sauce, 163
Noodles
    Red Cabbage with Sake on Rice Noodles,
        122
    Thai Noodles with Chili and Lemon Grass
        Dressing, 118–19
Nut spreads, 11
Nutrition, vegan diet and, 5–8
Nuts, 10
    Coriander Spiced, 19
    Spiced, 18

❖ o
Oils, 11
Olives
    Blood Oranges with Red Onions, Black Olives, and
        Fennel Dressing, 47
    with Fresh Rosemary and Orange, 22
    Grilled Eggplant with Black Olive Dressing, 94
    Mediterranean Potatoes with Olives, Herbs and
        Tomatoes, 150
    Warm Couscous with Garlic, Black Olives and
        Tomatoes, 67
Onions
    Blood Oranges with Red Onions, Black Olives, and
        Fennel Dressing, 47
    Four-Onion Croustades, 80
    Griddled Red Onion Slices with Couscous, 66
    Roasted Apple, Onion and Sweet Potato Soup,
        50–51

Roasted Red Onions and Wilted Spinach with
    Sweet Potatoes, 167
Sticky Golden Onion Tarts, 139
Oranges
    Baked Bananas with Oranges and Hazelnuts, 207
    Caramelized Oranges with Cranberries, 199
    Nectarine and Berry Crisp, 201
    Orange and Passion Fruit Sorbet, 188–89
    Orange Custard with Cherry Jam, 200

❖ p
Pacific Rim Coconut Curry, 164–65
Pakoras, Chili with Chunky Tomato Chutney, 30–31
Pancakes, 202
Pantry, stocking the, 9–13
Papaya
    and Cilantro Salsa on Coconut Rice, 91
    Coconut Rice Pudding with Mango and Papaya,
        181
    and Coconut Sherbet, 190–91
    Fresh Fruit in Wine with Basil, 196
Parsley
    and Garlic Pita Toasts, 34
    Mashed Potatoes, 90
    Shortcakes, 88–89
Parsnips
    Roasted Potatoes and Parsnips with Chestnuts and
        Sage, 96
    Vegetable Chips, 25
Passion Fruit Sorbet, Orange and, 188–89
Pasta, 11
    Bright Red Pepper Pesto Linguine, 68
    Fresh Ginger and Basil Pasta, 69
    Gnocchi with Tomatoes and Fresh Mint, 113
    Individual Crispy Porcini Bakes, 168–69
    Mixed Mushrooms and Tofu Pasta, 114–15
    Rich Mushroom Sauce with Tagliatelle, 73
    Roast Vine Tomatoes and Pasta, 72
    Roasted Garlic and Walnut Linguine, 117
    Spaghetti with Tomato Sauce, 116
    Summer Pasta Salad, 70–71
    Tomato and Pine Nut Linguine with Caramelized
        Lemon, 112
    Vegan Lasagna, 174–75
    Vivid Beet with Horseradish Gnocchi, 74
Pastes, 12
Pastry, 15
    See also Tarts
    Mediterranean Galette, 78
    Samosas with Mango Chutney, 76–77
Peaches
    Balsamic White Peach Salad with Parsley
        Shortcakes, 88–89
    Caramelized Peach and Almond Tart, 203
    Fruit with Cardamom and Vanilla, 187
    Peach and Lemon Grass Chutney, 146–47
    Poached Fruit in Lavender-Infused Syrup with
        Toffee Crisps, 186
    Potato Cakes with Peach and Lemon Grass
        Chutney, 146–47
Pears
    Apple and Pear Crisp, 201

Baked Pears and Ginger, 184
Hot Poached Pears with Toffee Crisps, 185
Modern Waldorf Salad, 101
Peas, 15
    New Potatoes and Small Peas with Pungent Green
        Sauce, 163
Pecan and Butternut Squash Tart, 204–5
Peppers and Zucchini with Balsamic Vinegar, Crispy
    Polenta, 166
Pesto Linguine, Bright Red Pepper, 68
Pita Bread with Garlic Cream and Fresh Lime, 104
Pizzas, Homemade, 176–77
Plum and Cinnamon Crisp, 201
Poached Fruit in Lavender-Infused Syrup with Toffee
    Crisps, 186
Polenta
    with Beans, 138
    Crispy Polenta Peppers and Zucchini with Balsamic
        Vinegar, 166
    Roasted Garlic Polenta with Sautéed Tomatoes,
        110–11
Popcorn, hot and spicy, 20
Potatoes
    with Broad Beans and Mint Vinaigrette, 48
    Eggplant and Potato Bake, 151
    Eggplant Butter with Sea Salt-Crusted Potatoes,
        160–61
    Garlic Mashed, 86–87
    Mediterranean Potatoes with Olives, Herbs and
        Tomatoes, 150
    Moroccan Spiced Red Potato with Chickpeas,
        148–49
    New Potatoes and Small Peas with Pungent Green
        Sauce, 163
    Pacific Rim Coconut Curry, 164–65
    Parsley Mashed, 90
    Potato Cakes with Peach and Lemon Grass
        Chutney, 146–47
    Puree of Beans and Potatoes with Olive Oil, 75
    Roasted Potatoes and Parsnips with Chestnuts and
        Sage, 96
    Rosemary Mashed, 84–85
    Spanish Potato Gratin, 95
Protein, 8
Puddings
    Coconut Rice Pudding with Mango and Papaya,
        181
    Moroccan Spiced Rice Pudding, 182–83
Pumpkin and Coconut Soup, Thai, 52
Puree of Beans and Potatoes with Olive Oil, 75
Pureed Avocado Dip with Pickled Ginger and Wasabi,
    23
Pureed Chickpeas with Stir-Fried Vegetables, 35

❖ r
Raspberries
    Apricot and Raspberry Cobbler, 215
    Chocolate Raspberry Hazelnut Cake, 214
    Frozen Yogurt Crunch with Raspberry Sauce, 195
Red Cabbage Relish with Parsley Mashed Potatoes, 90
Red Cabbage with Sake on Rice Noodles, 122
Refrigerator, stocking the, 13–14

Relish
    Red Cabbage, 90
    Tomato, 106
Rice, 11
    Basmati and Wild Rice Salad, 99
    Caramelized Fennel and Shallot Risotto, 124
    Coconut, 91
    Coconut Rice Pudding with Mango and Papaya,
        181
    Coriander Basmati, 142–43
    Japanese Rice Bowl with Vegetables, 126–27
    Moroccan Pilaf, 125
    Moroccan Spiced Rice Pudding, 182–83
    Saffron, 172–73
    Spring Vegetables with Saffron Basmati Rice,
        128–29
    Tomato and Basil Risotto, 123
Rich Mushroom Sauce with Tagliatelle, 73
Rich Mushrooms on Toast with Truffle Oil, 42
Risotto. See Rice
Roast Vine Tomatoes and Pasta, 72
Roasted Apple, Onion and Sweet Potato Soup, 50–51
Roasted Baby Zucchini, 21
Roasted Garlic and Walnut Linguine, 117
Roasted Garlic Polenta with Sautéed Tomatoes, 110–11
Roasted Potatoes and Parsnips with Chestnuts and
    Sage, 96
Roasted Red Onions and Wilted Spinach with Sweet
    Potatoes, 167
Roasted Squash Soup with Fresh Cilantro, 59
Roasted Vegetables with Couscous and Lemon Pepper
    Oil, 144–45

❖ s
Salads
    Balsamic White Peach Salad with Parsley
        Shortcakes, 88–89
    Basmati and Wild Rice Salad, 99
    Modern Waldorf Salad, 101
    Salad of Ciabatta Croutons with Avocado,
        Grapefruit and Vinaigrette, 97
    Summer Pasta Salad, 70–71
    Winter Fruit Salad, 218
    Winter Green Salad with Very Garlicky Vinaigrette,
        100
Salsa, 14
    Cilantro, 54
    Fruit, 180
    Papaya and Cilantro, 91
    Watercress, 40–41
Salt, 12
Samosas with Mango Chutney, 76–77
Sandwiches
    Avocado Butter with Tomato Relish in Focaccia,
        106
    Carrots with Mint and Lime Dressing in Pita
        Bread, 107
    Pita Bread with Garlic Cream and Fresh Lime, 104
    Thai Vegetables in Fresh Herb Bread, 105
Satay on White Bread, Spicy, 98
Sauces, 12
    Apple and Brandy Sauce, 210–11

Apricot, 216–17
Chili, 134–35
Pungent Green Sauce, 163
Red Wine and Mint Sauce, 27
Rich Mushroom Sauce with Tagliatelle, 73
Tomato, 92–93, 116
Scones with Fruit Salsa, Warm Hazelnut, 180
Seaweed, 12
Seeds, 10
Sherbets
Lemon Sherbet Cups with Crushed Blueberries, 194
Papaya and Coconut Sherbet, 190–91
Shortcakes, Parsley, 88–89
Sorbets, 15
Orange and Passion Fruit Sorbet, 188–89
Tomato, 55
Soups
Corn, Coconut, Lime and Basil Soup, 56–57
Creamy Carrot and Ginger Soup with Curly Toasts, 53
Roasted Apple, Onion and Sweet Potato Soup, 50–51
Roasted Squash Soup with Fresh Cilantro, 59
Spicy Gazpacho Soup with Paprika Croutons, 60–61
Thai Pumpkin and Coconut Soup, 52
Tomato Soup with Cilantro Salsa, 54–55
Vegetable Stock, 62
Wild Mushroom Soup, 58
Soy milk/cream, 14
Spaghetti with Tomato Sauce, 116
Spanish Potato Gratin, 95
Spiced Nuts, 18
Spices, 12
Spicy Gazpacho Soup with Paprika Croutons, 60–61
Spicy Satay on White Bread, 98
Spicy Vegetable Rounds with Chunky Tomato Chutney, 170–71
Spicy Vegetables and Coconut Cream, 130–31
Spinach
Balti, 154–55
Roasted Red Onions and Wilted Spinach with Sweet Potatoes, 167
Vegan Lasagna, 174–75
Warm Cumin and Coriander Spinach on Garlic Mashed Potatoes, 86–87
Spirits, 16
Sponge Cake with Strawberries and Lemon Balm, 212–13
Spring Rolls with Dipping Sauce, Chilied, 136–37
Spring Vegetables with Saffron Basmati Rice, 128–29
Squash
Pecan and Butternut Squash Tart, 203
Roasted Squash Soup with Fresh Cilantro, 59
Starters, 18–62
Steamed Bok Choy with Soy Sauce and Toasted Seeds, 29
Sticky Golden Onion Tarts, 139
Stir-Fried Black Beans with Lime and Chili, 156–57
Stock, vegetable, 13, 62

Strawberries
with Black Pepper, 197
Fresh Fruit in Wine with Basil, 196
Sponge Cake with Strawberries and Lemon Balm, 212–13
Sugars, 12
Summer Pasta Salad, 70–71
Sushi, with Avocado and Cucumber, Vegan, 120–21
Sweet potatoes
Hot Grilled Sweet Potato with Watercress Salsa, 40–41
Roasted Apple, Onion and Sweet Potato Soup, 50–51
Roasted Red Onions and Wilted Spinach with Sweet Potatoes, 167
Spicy Vegetable Rounds with Chunky Tomato Chutney, 170–71
Vegetable Chips, 25

❖ t
Tahini Dip, Lemon, 24
Tarts
Caramelized Peach and Almond Tart, 203
Fennel and Ginger, 79
Pecan and Butternut Squash Tart, 203
Sticky Golden Onion, 139
Treacle Tart, 206
Tuscan, 140
Thai Green Vegetable Curry, 158–59
Thai Noodles with Chili and Lemon Grass Dressing, 118–19
Thai Pumpkin and Coconut Soup, 52
Thai Vegetables in Fresh Herb Bread, 105
Toffee Crisps, 186
Toffee Figs with a Glass of Brandy, 198
Tofu Pasta, Mixed Mushrooms and, 114–15
Tomatoes
Chunky Tomato Chutney, 170–71
Crunchy Baked Tomatoes with Lime, Onion, and Chili, 44
Fried Tomato Toasts, 46
Roast Vine Tomatoes and Pasta, 72
Roasted Garlic Polenta with Sautéed Tomatoes, 110–11
Sorbet, 55
Tomato and Basil Risotto, 123
Tomato and Pine Nut Linguine with Caramelized Lemon, 112
Tomato Relish, 106
Tomato Sauce, 116
Tomato Soup with Cilantro Salsa, 54–55
Warm Couscous with Garlic, Black Olives and Tomatoes, 67
Warm Tomato and Eggplant Stacks, 82–83
Treacle Tart, 206
Tuscan Tarts, 140

❖ v
Vegan diet
choosing a, 1–2
nutrition and, 5–8
Vegan Lasagna, 174–75

Vegan margarine, 14
Vegan Sushi with Avocado and Cucumber, 120–21
Vegetables, 14
    Balti, 154–55
    in a Crispy Chickpea Batter, 32–33
    Grilled Vegetables on Lemon Grass Sticks with
        Coriander Basmati, 142–43
    Indian Vegetables, 152–53
    Japanese Rice Bowl with Vegetables, 126–27
    Juma's Special African Curry, 132–33
    Malaysian Vegetables, 141
    Pureed Chickpeas with Stir-Fried Vegetables, 35
    Roasted Vegetables with Couscous and Lemon
        Pepper Oil, 144–45
    Spicy Vegetable Rounds with Chunky Tomato
        Chutney, 170–71
    Spicy Vegetables and Coconut Cream, 130–31
    Spring Vegetables with Saffron Basmati Rice,
        128–29
    Thai Green Vegetable Curry, 158–59
    Thai Noodles with Chili and Lemon Grass
        Dressing, 118–19
    Thai Vegetables in Fresh Herb Bread, 105
    Vegetable Chips, 25
    Vegetable Stock, 13, 62
Vinegar, 13
Vitamins, 6
Vivid Beet with Horseradish Gnocchi, 74

❖ W

Waldorf Salad, Modern, 101
Walnuts
    Modern Waldorf Salad, 101

Roasted Garlic and Walnut Linguine, 117
    Walnut Layer with Apple and Brandy Sauce,
        210–11
Warm Butter Bean Puree, 36–37
Warm Couscous with Garlic, Black Olives and
    Tomatoes, 67
Warm Cumin and Coriander Spinach on Garlic
    Mashed Potatoes, 86–87
Warm Hazelnut Scones with Fruit Salsa, 180
Warm Lemon and Olive Oil Beans on Rosemary
    Mashed Potatoes, 84–85
Warm Tomato and Eggplant Stacks, 82–83
Wasabi, 16
    Pureed Avocado Dip with Pickled Ginger and
        Wasabi, 23
Watercress Salsa, 40–41
Wild Mushroom Soup, 58
Wines, 16
Winter Fruit Salad, 218
Winter Green Salad with Very Garlicky Vinaigrette,
    100
Wontons with Chili Sauce, 134–35

❖ Y

Yogurt Crunch with Raspberry Sauce, Frozen, 195

❖ Z

Zucchini
    Crispy Polenta Peppers and Zucchini with Balsamic
        Vinegar, 166
    Roasted Baby, 21
    Spicy Vegetable Rounds with Chunky Tomato
        Chutney, 170–71